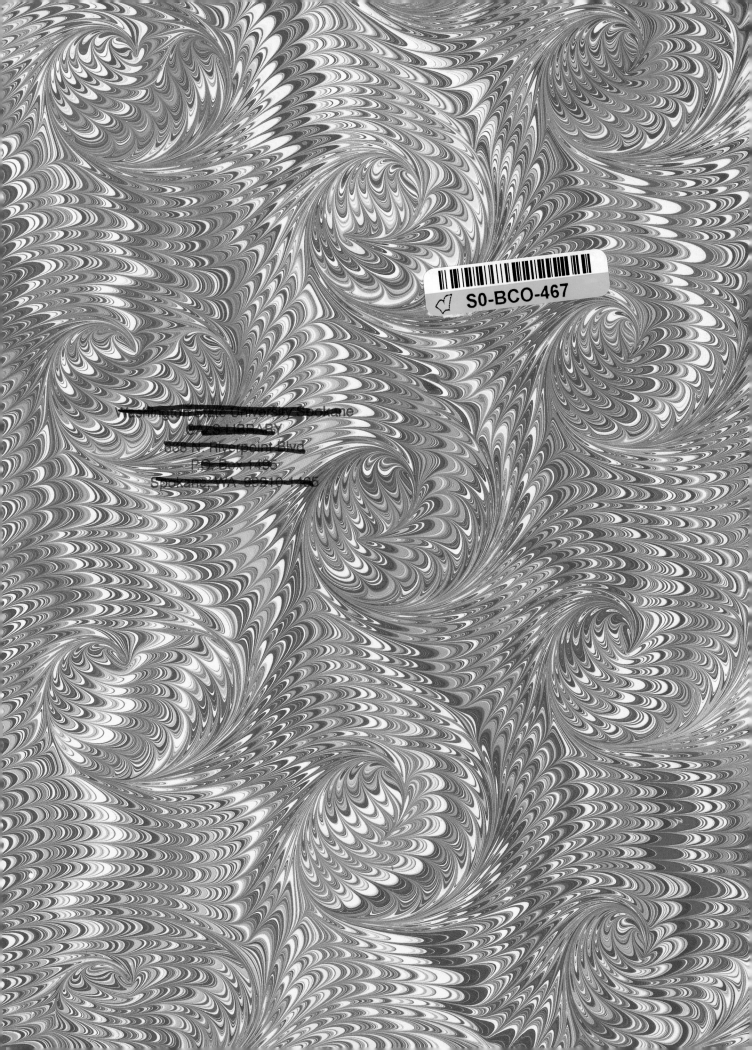

Knoll™ Furniture
1 9 3 8 - 1 9 6 0

Steven & Linda Rouland

Schiffer Publishing Ltd ®

4880 Lower Valley Road, Atglen, PA 19310 USA

Dedication

This book is dedicated to Donald Brooks-Miller.

Acknowledgments

The authors thank Knoll, Inc., for the use of their trademark and access to research materials. In particular, our thanks go to Albert Pfeiffer, curator of the Knoll Museum, who was generous with his time and always helpful in supplying material and answering our inquiries by letter, phone, or fax.

Our thanks go to Jennifer Komar Olivarez, Assistant Curator in the Department of Decorative Arts, Sculpture, and Architecture at the Minneapolis Institute of Arts. Pamela Lucas, Special Collections Librarian at the Grand Rapids Public Librar, who went above and beyond the call of duty; and Linda Aylward at the Peoria Public Library for saving us valuable time. Also, Chris Kennedy of DESIGNbase for supplying early materials.

Special thanks to David Vogel, of Atomic Interiors in Madison, Wisconsin, for providing valuable insights into the Knoll company and Paul Friling for his critical reading of the text and his appreciation of modern design. Mom (Marie Stankus) was always willing to work at the store on short notice, which helped immeasurably. And thank you to our family and friends who endured our no-shows at family events and get-togethers while we worked on the book.

Book Design by Anne Davidsen
Type set in Futura / Humanist

ISBN: 0-7643-0937-4

Printed in China
1 2 3 4

Published by Schiffer Publishing Ltd.
4880 Lower Valley Road
Atglen, PA 19310
Phone: (610) 593-1777; Fax: (610) 593-2002
E-mail: Schifferbk@aol.com
Please visit our web site catalog at
www.schifferbooks.com

This book may be purchased from the publisher.
Include $3.95 for shipping.
Please try your bookstore first.
We are interested in hearing from authors
with book ideas on related subjects.
You may write for a free catalog.

In Europe, Schiffer books are distributed by
Bushwood Books
6 Marksbury Rd.
Kew Gardens
Surrey TW9 4JF England
Phone: 44 (0)181 392-8585; Fax: 44 (0)181 392-9876
E-mail: Bushwd@aol.com

Contents

History and Designers

The Early Years

"We weren't making history," Florence Knoll said, "we were making design.[1]"
And yet, Knoll™ has a permanent place in the history of modern furniture design for the classics it produced. Mies van der Rohe and his Barcelona chair...Harry Bertoia and his wire chairs...and Eero Saarinen and his womb chair which was designed when Florence Knoll told him that she wanted a chair "like a big basket of pillows that I can curl up in."[2] From the beginning, Knoll was dedicated to design excellence, quality materials, and affordability. "No compromise, ever"[3] was their promise.

Hans G. Knoll Furniture Company

Hans G. Knoll, founder of Knoll Furniture Company, was born in 1914 in Germany to a family of furniture makers; his father, Walter Knoll, was a manufacturer of "modern" furniture. Hans was raised in Stuttgart and trained in the family business. He worked for Jantzen Knitting Mills in England for two years and, in 1935, started work for Plan Ltd., a company that did business with his father. By 1938 he was in New York where he established himself as the Hans G. Knoll Furniture Company at East 72nd Street. On the door he hung a sign proclaiming this as "Factory No. 1."

The first company catalog was made in 1942 from cardboard. Of the twenty-five items listed there, fifteen were designed by Jens Risom. At the time, Risom designed for Knoll on a royalty basis and collaborated with him on other projects prior to his going to war in 1943. Two of these projects were the press lounge, for the General Motors exhibit, and a "living kitchen" in the "America at Home" exhibit at the New York World's Fair.[4] By the time Risom returned from the war in 1945, things had changed at Knoll. Florence Schust had arrived on the scene.

Hans Knoll with a Bertoia sculpture in his office, as pictured in Knoll Design.

Patented July 10, 1945   Des. 141,839

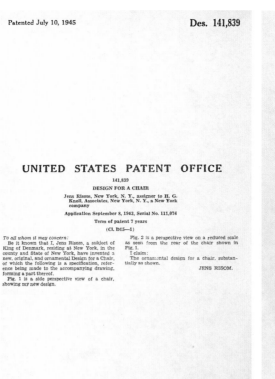

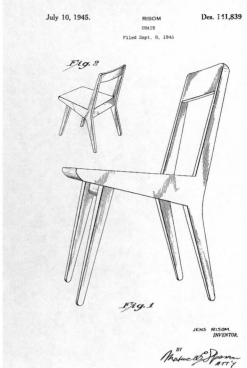

July 10, 1945.   RISOM   Des. 141,839
CHAIR
Filed Sept. 8, 1943

Patent filed in 1943 by Jens Risom on the 666 Chair.

Florence Knoll

Florence Knoll (neé Florence Schust) was interested in architecture and design from her early years. After visiting several schools, "Shu" chose to attend Kingswood, a girls' school that was designed as part of the Cranbrook Academy by Eliel Saarinen, who was head of the Cranbrook Academy of Art a the time. Saarinen noticed the interest young Shu took in the buildings of the school and encouraged her interest in architecture. She was treated as a member of the Saarinen family and accompanied them on a vacation trip to Finland. Eliel's son, Eero, later would design for Knoll.

Florence Schust studied in England at the Architectural Association in London, the world's oldest school of architecture. She returned to the United States to complete her training at the Armour Institute (Illinois Institute of Technology) where Mies van der Rohe was the professor of architecture. In an interview published in *The New York Times*, she said that she "learned more from him than from anyone, and in fewer words."[5] Knoll would later produce a number of designs by van der Rohe.

Knoll Associates

By 1943, Florence was working for Hans Knoll, taking on extra jobs on a part-time basis as her time permitted. The two formed Knoll Associates and were married in 1946.[6] Florence was a full partner in the business, an unusual arrangement at that time. She headed the Knoll Planning Unit and was in charge of interior design. During the forties, Knoll worked with designers Pierre Jeanneret, Abel Sorenson, Franco Albini, Hans Bellman, and Ralph Rapson, among others.

The early years were a struggle, but the Knolls were determined to succeed. Hans had skills the young firm needed: he was very good with people and had a natural ability for sales. As described by Murray Rothenberg, a Knoll employee, "Hans was a superlative salesman. He could sell almost anything. He was always selling—himself, his product, the company. You would do anything for him. He had the ability to get you to work for him. You would also hate his guts sometimes."[7] Knoll's dedication to his young company was absolute and he invested all of his time and talents into making Knoll Associates successful.

Hans relied on Florence a great deal. She had an extraordinary talent for design which Hans was quick to utilize. They were in agreement that they wanted Knoll Associates to become something special. Between them they had a great number of contacts and the idea was born to bring outside talent to Knoll Associates. They would have their own Planning Unit designers as well as purchase free-lance designs. Hans said, "It was my whole idea to develop new products working with well-know designers, and to encourage their particular talents."[8] Eero Saarinen, Isamu Noguchi, Harry Bertoia, and many other talented artisans designed for Knoll Associates. The company bought the designs, manufactured and distributed the product but the Knolls had decided early on to give credit to the designers and pay them royalties.

The Knolls were dedicated to establishing a firm where designers could create and achieve their full potential. For example, "The Knolls staked Harry Bertoia, the sculptor, to two years in a studio barn in Pennsylvania to see if, after his work with metals, he could turn out furniture. His wire chairs were the answer," as quoted from *The New York Times*.[9] Knoll Associates produced this line in 1952. Essentially an artist, these were the only furniture pieces Bertoia would ever produce.

Another designer who worked for Knoll Associates in the early years was Richard Schultz. As he said, "...in those days I don't think anyone thought about money because everybody loved Knoll. Most of them could have made more money someplace else, but Hans used to pat you on the back. You'd get to the point where you were going to quit, and he'd come and pat you on the back and you felt so great that didn't have to give you a raise."[10] The charismatic Hans and the talented Shu were making Knoll Associates the place to be for designers.

It was also their idea that Knoll would be dedicated to the production of *exclusively modern designs*. Other firms might produce a modern line along with traditional furniture, but Knoll was determined to sink or swim with modern. This dedication was borne out as the company name became synonymous with the term *modern*. Indeed, a *Life* magazine article hailed them as "The Drum Beaters of Modern."

Once they gathered the talent, they had to produce the products, and this was not so easy while there were still material shortages caused by the war restrictions and quality issues with the materials that were available. "During World War II, when materials for furniture and decorative fabrics were difficult to procure, the firm's designers used wood and metal scraps to create stools and chairs; they turned to tweeds when the more usual textiles had high military priority;

The entrance lobby of Connecticut General, as pictured in *Knoll Design*.

they converted Army-rejected parachute belting into webbing for lightweight chairs; and, in order to save on scarce lumber, they designed slanting drawer fronts which did not require handles. In this way new materials and new techniques contributed to the creation of modern designs and original methods of production."[11]

The Knolls had contacts among would-be clients as well. Hans was always able to get business for the firm. An introduction from a friend led to their first major assignment, the Rockefeller family offices in Rockefeller Plaza. "That was starting at the top!" said Florence Knoll.[12] With that type of assignment as their calling card, the Knolls had arrived.

While modern buildings were being built, and older buildings were redesigned, there were no modern interiors to complement them. Architects were designing buildings, yet the interiors of those buildings were usually a hodge-podge of styles. There was, as Florence Knoll would say, a "conflict" between the buildings external appearance and internal space. Florence Knoll was one of the first to carefully consider the entire picture, including the building itself.

In the early fifties, the architectural firm Skidmore, Owings & Merrill gave the Knolls a chance to apply their approach on a large scale. They recommended Knoll Associates to design offices, cafeterias, lobbies and recreation spaces for 2,000

Lounge area at Connecticut General, as pictured in *Knoll Design*

The New York showroom's brightly colored panels set off the furniture displayed there. As pictured in *Interiors* Magazine, May, 1951.

employees in a complex of buildings for the Connecticut General Life Insurance Company in Bloomfield, Connecticut. Florence Knoll carefully assessed the use of the existing space and interviewed the employees before deciding how to proceed. Colors, fabrics, and, of course, furniture all were carefully considered. The assignment went extremely well and set a precedent for interior design on a large scale.

Knoll Showrooms and Offices

The Knolls used their showrooms and offices to "speak" for them. Clients sometimes had to be pursuaded; the modern aesthete was not universally embraced. Fortunately, "...Knoll spoke to an audience of forward-thinking connoisseurs who appreciated the statements an avante-garde might be making but whose preferences were too refined to buy anything ridiculous."[13] Many clients became believers once they saw those interiors. The showrooms and offices allowed Knoll to demonstrate what they could do with color, fabric, and of course, furniture.

In 1951 Knoll Associates moved to new headquarters on the fourteenth floor at 575 Madison Avenue in New York, and Florence Knoll directed the redesign of the interior space. An article from *Interiors* magazine tells us how there was a "malicious smacking of lips"[14] over this move. It was anticipated that this was a design challenge Florence Knoll might not be able to handle. The building itself had architectural oddities such as very low ceilings, off-kilter walls, and a view that was no view at all, but only steel and concrete.

Florence Knoll rose to the challenge with stunning results. She had frames of hollow, black tubes built from which panels could be suspended down a wall or across a ceiling, tricking the eye into thinking the ceiling floated somewhere above the panels. These panels, some of which were colorful and some transparent, created the dimensions she wanted for each area, and most of them were movable. The hollow tubes also served as conduits for the lighting fixtures. Thick, white, fiberglass fishnet panels screened out the concrete "views," while permitting filtered light to enter the space. A black panel was thrown in capriciously (she loved to play with color). Even the restroom doors, which opened into the showroom, received a novel touch; door handles were removed and the entire wall was paneled. Two bright stripes of color marked the location of hidden finger holds for the doors; until someone actually used the doors, no one knew they were there.

To this setting, she added the furniture and accessories. A Mies van der Rohe grouping greeted visitors in the first setting, while a reflecting pool greeted visitors in the next. Each setting had a different treatment. Calder mobiles, sculptures by Bertoia, and paintings by Miro and Klee contributed to the open feeling.

The Knolls were equally fastidious about the design of their own offices. Hans's office was only twelve feet square in size, but was very striking. It featured a black wall behind the desk, a color Florence chose to highlight Hans's ruddy complexion, and bamboo blinds and raw silk curtains to match the color of his hair.

Light filtered in from a large side window, giving the office the illusion of much larger space than it actually was. This office was

Hans Knoll's office, designed by Florence Knoll. From *Interiors* Magazine May 1951.

Showroom with reflecting pool surprised visitors. Photo mural of an old French loom adds another dramatic flourish. From *Interiors* Magazine May 1951.

used to educate clients just as much as the showrooms were. Florence's office appeared more functional. Fabric samples covered part of one wall, while the windowsill behind her desk contained some of the models and mockups she loved to use. The models included "...a familiar Saarinen chair, a checker boarded marble cube, a sculptured metal cloud by Harry Bertoia, and a bowl of flowers normal size" as described in *Interiors* magazine.[15]

As Knoll Associates business expanded, showrooms were built in cities as diverse as Los Angeles, Stuttgart, Dallas, and Milan. By 1955, Chicago, Detroit, Miami, Boston, Brussels, Stockholm, Zurich, and Toronto all had Knoll showrooms. The one thing they all had in common was the very visual, very colorful Knoll style which was such a fitting backdrop for the furniture the company produced. Some would call it "International Style."

Knoll International & Knoll Textiles

The company continued to grow during the early 1950s, mirroring the growth of the American economy. Manufacturing facilities were established in East Greenville, Pennsylvania, and in Europe. Even though Knoll was grossing over $3 million in sales by this time, furniture and textiles were made "on demand" for the client, and mostly by hand. Hans focused on the manufacturing end of the business while Florence Knoll continued working with the design of office space. Hans was soon able to realize his dream to grow the company globally and have more interaction with overseas designers, as he had had with Albini and others in the early days.

Knoll International was formed in 1951 as a result of a United States State Department request to make furniture for American personnel stationed overseas. Florence recalled, in *Knoll Design*, that she was never quite sure how they got the contract, however "...this was just the kind of thing Hans was good at."[16] They started operations in Europe, adding locations that were exotic: Africa, Karachi, Libya, and Tripoli. American embassies in Copenhagen, Stockholm and Havana were also furnished by Knoll. By 1964, Knoll had truly gone global with twenty-one overseas offices, numerous showrooms, and many licensees selling Knoll products.

In the Dallas showroom, color was used to define space. As pictured in *Interiors* Magazine July 1957.

Knoll Textiles

A textiles division, called Knoll Textiles, was formed because Florence was not satisfied with available fabrics. She even used men's suiting cloth as upholstery. Textiles had their own showroom on East 65th Street in New York as early as 1947.

Eszter Haraszty headed the textile division in the early 1950s when textiles designs were woven by hand or printed on fabric. Marianne Strengel, who had been in charge of the weaving studios at Cranbrook, designed drapery and upholstery fabrics for Knoll and acted as a consultant. Anni Albers was another designer for the textiles division.

Textiles became an integral part of Knoll's products. While there was a predilection to hand weaving, some materials were produced on power looms to make them available to a wider audience. Evelyn Hill was one designer whose handwoven work was reproduced on a power loom. Beautiful as well as durable, these fabrics added to Knoll's success. Eventually, Knoll Textiles would sell directly to the trade, augmenting their in-house production.

Knoll's textiles won many design awards during the 1950's, such as the Museum of Modern Art, Good Design Award, 1951, for "Knoll Stripes" by Eszter Haraszty. Eszter won again in 1953 for "Fibra." Florence Knoll would use "Fibra" for the curtains in the CBS building interiors she would later design. More awards followed for designs with names like: "Diamonds", "Pythagoras", "Lazy Lines", and "Triad."

"Transportation Cloth" was an award winner in 1951; as the name implies, it was used for planes, trains, and buses. Another commercial success was "Knoll Nylon Homespun."

Florence Knoll had a personal dislike for prints, she preferred textiles and color to add interest to walls. She used the textiles Knoll produced for the Planning Unit she headed. One in particular, "Pandanus", was so often used that it became a symbol for Knoll.

Walls were painted two tone in the Dallas showroom to create more visual interest. As pictured in *Interiors* Magazine, July, 1957.

FOUR KNOLL WINNERS

FIRST AWARD—printed fabrics
"Fibra" by Eszter Haraszty
FIRST AWARD—printed fabrics
"Fibra" on sheer by Eszter Haraszty
FIRST AWARD, woven fabrics
"Linen Casement" by Eszter Haraszty
HONORABLE MENTION—woven fabrics
"Kerry Linen" by Evelyn Hill

American Institute of Decorators 1953 Home Furnishings Design Competition

Swatches are available upon request

KNOLL TEXTILES INC., 575 MADISON AVE., N.Y. 22 • BOSTON, CHICAGO, DALLAS, DETROIT, MIAMI, WASHINGTON

Award winning fabrics from Knoll Textiles.

The End of an Era

The fifties, which were a time of expansion for Knoll, also saw the death of its founder. Hans died in a car accident in 1955 at the age of 41. Characteristically, he was on business for Knoll, visiting the offices of Knoll International in Cuba.

"Hans Knoll has made a great and lasting contribution to the cultural world," Eero Saarinen wrote at the time, "No one has done so much to change the interiors of our buildings....He always freely gave credit to his designers, yet he who played a big part in their work, never took any credit himself. The generosity, the enthusiasm, the inspiration and concern for human beings which he brought to everything he touched will long be remembered by all of us."[17]

Florence Knoll was now the president of Knoll Associates, Knoll Textiles, and Knoll International. She continued to oversee the company's growth and development. She sold the companies to Art Metal Inc., but remained as president until 1960. For the next five years, she continued working as a consultant for Knoll. In 1958, Florence Knoll remarried, becoming Florence Knoll Bassett. She and her husband lived on Sunset Island, near Miami, and kept an apartment in New York, allowing her easy access to the Knoll offices when she was in town.

Her last major commission was for the Columbia Broadcasting System(CBS). Eero Saarinen had designed the building and had intended to design the interiors as well. He died before doing so, and CBS turned to Mrs. Bassett for help. The building was a tall, black, granite skyscraper, 38 stories high, capable of housing 2,700 people.

A CBS vice presidents office shows off Mrs. Bassett's use of color. From *Knoll Design*.

Some of the ground work for the interiors had been done, so she did not entirely have a free hand. She was essentially to step in and complete a work that had been in progress. She did so, creating pleasant work areas, and high individualized corporate suites. The employee cafeteria-lounge, called the 51/20 Club, she had some fun with. It was dominated by a huge mural covering an entire wall, consisting of words associated with food. That "gastrotypographicalassemblage" was created by Lou Dorfsman, director of Design at CBS. In her own discussion of her work, Florence would use words like "unity" and "harmony." As always, she sought to reconcile the exterior space with the interior. Her use of color sets her work apart.

"That job was a tour de force for her, and I have always felt that she recognized that before others did. It made a spectacular exit line for a brilliant career," said her assistant, Christine Rae.[18]

Florence's retirement in 1965 marked the end of an era for Knoll. By that time, the company had design credits that included 250 executive offices for the Alcoa building in Pittsburgh, a 600 room dormitory for the University of Michigan at Ann Arbor, the Art Gallery at Yale University, the Virginia Museum of Fine Arts, the Saarinen building housing the Columbia Broadcasting System (CBS), the Rockefeller family offices, offices of the U.S. Veterans Administration, and U.S. embassies overseas. It was an impressive roster.

Knoll after the Knolls

Knoll continued to carry on its tradition of design successes. The company used a two-pronged approach. First, create the design and approve it based on the merits of appearance, function, and appeal (or, buy the design if it meets these criteria). Second, figure out how to produce it. This was the case with a line designed by Warren Platner that Florence Knoll had purchased prior to her retirement.

As with the Bertoia chairs, Platner's were steel wire. Platner used parallel lines, a graceful form but difficult to produce. A special electric welder had to be used to conjure up the final product. Another production problem had been solved, but Knoll was about to enter an era when the old methods of manufacture would be replaced by the methods of mass production.

Other furniture designs that were introduced during this time include Richard Schultz' "Leisure Collection", Charles Pollack's "Sling" lounge chair and Don Albinson's stacking chairs.

In 1968 Knoll purchased the Gavina Company. The Gavina Company was a mecca for aspiring European designers. Through the Gavina Company, Knoll acquired the talents of designers like Roberto Sebastian Matta, Tobia Scarpa, Kazuhide Takahama, and Vico Magistretti. Knoll also acquired the license to manufacture designs by Marcel Breuer. Breuer's Wassily chair (designed in 1925) was produced in 1969 by Knoll, as well as other designs.

Knoll was formally recognized for its contribution to modern furniture design when the Louvre Museum hosted an exhibition, called Knoll au Louvre, in Paris. The exhibition ran from January 12 to March 12, 1972, and featured the design classics for which the company was known. Florence Knoll Bassett was able to attend, as were some of the Knoll designers. It was a tribute that would have been appreciated by Hans Knoll, and received very favorable reviews from the European press.

A design evolution was taking place during the 1970s. The work of Morrison and Hannah, with its rounded edges and soft cushions, spoke to a new age of comfort. Even though this was a different vision for Knoll, it was only natural that Knoll should produce this new style. Knoll's directive had always been to produce excellence in modern design. As Morrison said, "Knoll was really the only place to go. Others at the time were still doing green cabinets."[19] Morrison and Hannah would win the Ventures Design award of the Aluminum Corporation for their lounge chair and high back sofa.

The 1967 Platner Collection.

Part of the Richard Schultz Leisure Collection.

Left: Malitte lounge seating designed by Roberto Sebastian Matta. Stackable blocks of foam rubber with wool upholstery. *Photo Courtesy of the Knoll Museum.*

Far Left: Arm chair designed by Tobia Scarpa introduced to the United States in 1969.

By 1973, the open office concept had taken hold. Walls were out and open office spaces were in. Knoll at this time launched an an open office line by one of their designers, Bill Stephens, called the Stephens System. It was a success in an industry experiencing tough times. Commercial office furniture production plummeted during the late 1970s and early 1980s as companies sought to trim their bottom line. The expansive days of the 1950s and 1960s were over.

Walter E. Heller, International, Chicago, acquired Art Metal and Knoll, in 1967-1968. The company became Knoll International in 1969, taking the name of its overseas division. The Planning Unit was disbanded in 1971 and staff morale was affected. The seventies were a difficult time for Knoll ideologically. Sales were down in 1970-1971. Heller, under a government-ordered divestiture, put Knoll up for sale.

Marshall Cogan and Stephen Swid bought (still privately held) Knoll in 1977, and it became a division of General Felt Industries, a floor covering manufacturer. Cogan and Swid, with experience as securities analysts, felt they could improve Knoll. They had earlier returned General Felt to profitability. They made more changes at Knoll, including a switch to mass manufacture. General Felt issued stock in Knoll as Knoll International in 1983, taking the company public.

Lounge chair designed by Morrison and Hannah.

In 1986, General Felt bought back the shares to once again make the company private. From the initial offering, $20 million was used to expand the East Greenville facility. During this time, Knoll began marketing its "KnollStudio" line, for use in the home as well as the office. The line included designs which had been in continuous production for years, by Breuer, Bertoia and others. The line was well received.

Westinghouse bought Knoll from General Felt in 1990 as well as furniture makers Shaw, Walker, and Reff, Inc. The companies were then combined to form a subsidiary of Westinghouse called the Knoll Group. The Knoll Group was now the third largest office furniture maker in the country, behind Steelcase and Herman Miller.

Warburg, Pincus Ventures, L.P. bought the Knoll Group from Westinghouse in 1996 for $565 million. In February of 1996, Knoll Group became Knoll, Inc. Subsidiaries of Knoll, Inc. include KnollStudio, KnollExtra, Knoll Textiles, and Spinneybeck. Knoll again went public in May of 1997, issuing shares traded on the New York Stock Exchange under the symbol "KNL."

Today, Knoll is a dynamic company, growing and changing as it must to remain an industry leader. Even as it grows away from its past, it has taken steps to preserve it by opening a company museum, located at the East Greenville facility. Here, a 48-foot time line of Knoll history stretches across a curved wall. Artifacts like a piece of glass from the original Brno House Barcelona table rest in display cases. Some of the models used in the design work are also shown. The furniture exhibited is, for the most part, no longer in production and the displays are rotated periodically. A goal of the museum is to further education by allowing objects to be loaned out to schools or other museums.

Knoll's classic designs have stood the test of time. For example, Saarinens' futuristic looking pedestal chairs and tables were used in the hit movie, Men in Black. Models in ads are often perched on Bertoia chairs or Tulip chairs, Knoll designs pop up everywhere.

Knoll is dedicated to continuing the rich tradition of design excellence it was imbued with by its founders. While acknowledging that history, Knoll looks forward to an even brighter future.

The Designers

Albini, Franco (1905-1977)

The words "architect, designer, and city planner" all describe Franco Albini. A graduate of the Milan Polytechnic Institute, he established his own studio in Milan, circa 1930. For a competition in 1933, he designed a transparent radio, using Perspex, a clear acrylic.

Albini is known for his plate glass and wire shelving, hung from suspended wires. His designs for Knoll include a glass topped desk and chairs with wooden or metal legs.

Albini's design credits also include the "La Rinascente" department store in Rome and the subway in Milan, Italy. He designed museum interiors such as the Brera in Milan and also designed for Brion Vega Radio and Television. He was among the earliest designers to be associated with Cassina, a modern Italian furniture manufacturer.

Bellman, Hans (b.1911-)

Hans Bellman studied engineering drafting in Baden from 1927 to 1930. He became a student of Mies van der Rohe at the Bauhaus in Dessau and Berlin in the early 1930s. He then worked in Mies office from 1933 to 1934. He worked with various architects before opening his own firm in Zurich in 1946. From 1948 to 1954 he taught at Kunstgewerbeschule in Zurich and at the Basel Allgemeine Gewerbeschule. He also taught at Harvard University and Washington University in Seattle.

His work for Knoll included a pair of tripod tables with white laminate tops and folding legs. He also designed a dining table for Knoll.

Floating desk and wire shelving designed by Franco Albini. A similar chair was produced by Knoll. As pictured in *Interiors* magazine July 1948.

Bertoia, Harry (b. Arieto Bertoia 1915-1978)

An American citizen, born in Italy, Bertoia was an artist, a sculptor, a jewelry maker, a designer, truly a "renaissance man." He studied and taught at Cranbrook, where he would meet Florence Knoll. In 1939, he set up a metal workshop there, making jewelry and other metal objects. When the war made metal scarce, Bertoia worked in the graphics department.

Bertoia left Cranbrook in 1943 and went to California. There, he worked with Charles and Ray Eames at Evans Products Company. The Eames had been working on a process to bend plywood for use in low cost furniture production and were using this new technology to produce leg splints and other products for the U.S. navy. After the war they turned their attention back to furniture design. Eames and Bertoia collaborated on a chair with a plywood seat and metal legs. Eames and Bertoia were not in agreement regarding the attribution of their work. Also, Eames was more interested in working with plywood whereas Bertoia was interested in metalwork. Bertoia left and began working for the Naval Electronics Laboratory, but hoped for something more in line with his interests. Fortunately, the Knolls sent him a letter requesting him to come and work for them. The arrangement with Knoll was conducive to the artist - work at what you will, and if a design for furniture comes out of your work, Knoll would produce the design.

From this arrangement would come Bertoia's classic metal chairs. The Knolls had a good relationship with Bertoia, but understandably were hoping that some thing productive would come from their association. After Bertoia had begun the work, Knoll sent Richard Schultz to help things along. "We just knew from the very beginning that these chairs were going to be extraordinary," he said in an interview, "I can remember feeling that I was working on something that was on a very high level."[20]

Bertoia experimented in open forms and metal work. The line of chairs he designed for Knoll were extensions of his art. "In the sculpture I am concerned primarily with space, form and the characteristics of metal. In the chairs many functional problems have to be established first...but when you get right down to it, the chairs are studies in space, form and metal too," he said.[21]

Knoll introduced Bertoia's "diamond chairs" in 1952. The chairs themselves were an open network of small diamonds which formed a large diamond, the chair itself. Made of thin metal rods, the chair was a challenge for Knoll to produce; each chair was made by hand. Covers were made for the chair, and Knoll also produced it in a children's size. Knoll's Bertoia chairs would enter the pantheon of modern design classics.

After designing his chairs, Bertoia worked primarily as a sculptor. He was interested in the relationship between sound and movement; his pieces sometimes produced percussive sounds and had moving parts. A major work was the sculpture done for the General Motors Technical Center in Detroit. Another Cranbrook friend, Eero Saarinen, often featured Bertoia sculptures in his buildings, notably at MIT in Cambridge and Dulles International Airport. Florence Knoll also used Bertoia sculptures in the showrooms she designed.

Bertoia was honored with many awards and his work was featured in art and furniture exhibitions worldwide, including Knoll au Louvre in Paris.

Bonet, Kurchan, and Hardoy

Jorge Ferrari-Hardoy, Antonio Bonet, and Juan Kurchan, were partners in an Argentine architectural firm and designed the Hardoy or Sling chair for use in their own offices. Their inspiration came from a wooden folding chair that was common in Europe. Knoll began production of the chair in 1947 under a licensing agreement with Hardoy. Copying the chair was painfully simple and knockoffs became so common that Knoll decided to file suit against one of the copiers as a test case. Knoll lost the case and discontinued the chair in 1950. It has been estimated that over five million Hardoy chairs have been produced.

Butler, Lewis

Lew Butler graduated with honors from Pratt University in Brooklyn, New York, in 1949. He was one of the first designers to come to Knoll specifically to work in the Planning Unit. He was senior designer and assistant to Florence Knoll from 1950-1965, and Planning Unit director from 1965-1970. Butler was involved in all major Planning Unit projects and designed several tables for Knoll along with a lounge chair and a sofa.

Harry Bertoia sculpture and Diamond chair with unique two-tone fabric.

Cafiero, Vincent

Vincent Cafiero graduated from the Pratt Institute in New York in 1952. After showing Florence Knoll what he called "the most incomplete portfolio ever presented,"[22] he went to work for the Planning Unit and was senior designer there from 1956-1967. He was special assistant to Florence Knoll from 1963-1965, attached to the Knoll Design Development Group. He worked on many of the major projects including CBS and Connecticut General. He designed the No.180 Arm Chair and worked in the development of Knoll library furniture and equipment. Cafiero said of Knoll, "What we were doing above all else was making beautiful furniture. We were taking the Bauhaus idea of design and development and making it a profitable operation."[23]

Jeanneret, Pierre (1896-1967)

Born in Switzerland, Pierre Jeanneret studied architecture in Geneva. Jeanneret was also a designer, painter, and town planner. He worked with Jean Prouvé designing prefabricated housing and helped Georges Blanchon with town planning for Puteaux, France.

Jeanneret joined the firm of his cousin, Le Corbusier, in the 1920s. They collaborated with Charlotte Perriand on furniture designs. Together with Le Corbusier, he designed government buildings in India. He is best known for his "No. 92, Scissor Chair," which Knoll produced.

Knoll, Florence (1917-)

Florence Knoll would become known as an interior designer and space planner par excellence. Trained as an architect, she also designed furniture and decorative objects. Her design and architectural studies began at a young age. Florence Knoll, then Florence Schust, attended Kingswood, a girls school at Cranbrook. There, she was noticed by Eliel Saarinen, the school's director. Saarinen encouraged her interest in architecture and the arts, and the orphaned "Shu" virtually became a part of the Saarinen family. Cranbrook offered a host of learning opportunities, and young Shu was exposed to crafts like weaving and pottery making along with more traditional studies.

While at Cranbrook, she would form associations with architects and designers who would later design for Knoll, including Eero Saarinen, Ralph Rapson, and Harry Bertoia. Her studies continued in Europe after leaving Cranbrook. She studied art and architecture at the Architectural Association in London before returning to the United States. She obtained her Bachelor of Architecture in 1941 after studying with Mies van der Rohe at the Illinois Institute of Technology, then known as the Armour Institute.

Her career began with her work for Walter Gropius and Marcel Breuer in Boston. Later she worked for architect Wallace K. Harrison in New York. By 1943, she had joined Knoll as director of the Planning Unit, in charge of design and the development of furniture and textiles. In 1946, she and Hans Knoll were married.

Florence Knoll as pictured in *Interiors* Magazine, July, 1957.

Florence Knoll obtained the rights for Knoll to produce (in 1948) the Barcelona chair and Tugendhat coffee table designed by her former teacher, Mies van der Rohe. Concurrently, Knoll produced the Womb chair of her former schoolmate, Eero Saarinen.

Florence Knoll also designed the furniture needed for the company's interior design projects. She did not attach much significance to her own work. As she says, "I designed the fill-in pieces that no one else was doing...Eero and Bertoia did the stars...I did it because I needed the piece of furniture for a job and it wasn't there, so I designed it."[24] Her "fill-in" pieces included desks, a "boat-shaped" conference table and a line of cabinets. Her cabinets could be either floor or wall mounted, and were widely copied. She also designed a sofa and chair group in 1954.

Like Mies van der Rohe, Florence Knoll also concerned herself with every detail. Everything came under her scrutiny, right down to door handles and ashtrays. She concerned herself with the space in its entirety and did not tolerate mediocrity.

Florence Knoll became known for the interiors done by the Knoll Planning Unit, which she headed until 1965. Architects found in her work interiors that would complement the exteriors they had designed. The interior spaces she designed have a rationality which came from her architectural training. The designs were crisp, clean, and elegant, earning the sobriquet "the Knoll look."

She was largely responsible for the acceptance by corporate America of that look. A 1964 New York Times article was titled "Woman Who Led an Office Revolution..."[25] During this interview, she talked about the "straightening of the cater-cornered desk" as her "single biggest struggle."

Executives invariably had this desk, usually massive, in their well "decorated" offices. Florence Knoll emphasized the difference between design and decoration. "I am not a decorator", she said.[26] She was an interior designer and space planner who was among the first to correlate a buildings interiors with its exterior, and to study the use of an office before designing for it. The design "revolution" she began in the 1940s reached its heyday in the 1960s.

After Hans Knoll died in 1955, Florence continued as President of Knoll. While designing the executive offices of the First National Bank in Miami, she met Harry Hood Bassett, whom she married in 1958. From this point, until her retirement in 1965, Florence Bassett would share her time between her home in Florida and her offices in New York.

Florence Knoll received many awards for her work, including the Good Design Award from 1950-1954, the AIA Gold Medal in 1961, and was inducted into the Hall of Fame at the Illinois Institute of Technology in 1982. Her work has also been featured in exhibitions in the United States and abroad.

Knorr, Don (1922-)

Don Knorr studied architecture at the University of Illinois and was a graduate student at Cranbrook. After Cranbrook, he worked for Eliel and Eero Saarinen before opening his own practice in San Francisco.

In 1949, Knorr shared first prize in the Museum of Modern Art's International Competition for Low-Cost Furniture in the seating category. Knoll agreed to manufacture the award winning chair. The original design of the chair seat called for quarter inch thermoset plastic bent to form a conical seat and back. In a small trial run Knoll found the new technology needed to make the seat was cost prohibitive. With Knorr's help, Knoll redesigned the chair, switching from plastic to sheet metal. However, in the end, this proved to be even more costly. In 1952, due to the Korean War, a restriction was placed on the gauge of metal being used. Due to these problems, the Knorr chair was discontinued.[27]

Matter, Herbert (1907-1984)

Known primarily for his photography, Matter was one of the first to apply this art form to marketing and advertising, as he did for Knoll. He studied painting in Paris during the 1920s, and worked with A.M Cassandre and Le Corbusier. A Swiss native, he did a series of posters for the Swiss National Tourist Office in the 1930s. The posters were visually striking, with objects and figures skillfully composed by Matter in a style known as photomontage.

Matter came to the United States in 1936 and designed the Swiss Pavilion and Corning Glass Pavilion for the 1939 New York World's Fair.

Matter worked for Knoll as a design and advertising consultant from 1946-1966. His ads for Knoll included the famous chimney sweep ad which ran in the New Yorker magazine for more than a decade. The ad shows a tired, grimy chimney sweep comfortably seated in a bright red Saarinen Womb chair. Another famous ad for Knoll showed his son, dressed as a cowboy, playing in a Hardoy chair. Matter simply let the boy play, shooting frame after frame, then laying out the multiple shots in the ad. Matter also used the Knolls sheepdog, Cartree, in some of the early ads with such success that other firms started using dogs in their ads as well.

Matter also designed the Knoll trademark, which started out as the word Knoll and then changed to a single large "K." Matter also used a seagull as a symbol for Knoll in both the advertising and showrooms.

While working for Knoll, Matter was also a photographer for Condé Nast Publications. He collaborated on the Knoll au Louvre catalog, and made a film titled The Works of Calder. He also served as advisor for institutions such as the Guggenheim Museum in New York. Matter was a Professor of Photography at Yale University from 1952-1982, where he trained many graphic designers.

Matters famous ad showing his son playing with the Hardoy chair.

Florence Knoll did not like this Herbert Matter advertisement (she thought it undignified) but Hans loved it.

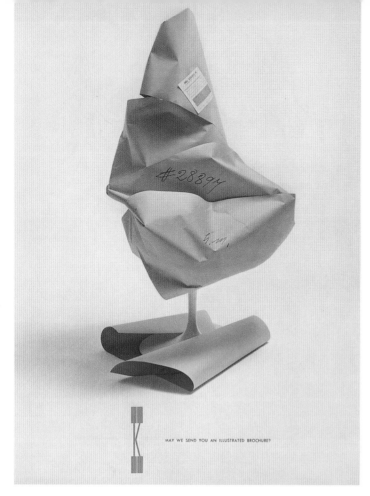

This brochure cover, designed by Matter, opened to reveal the unwrapped chair and a pretty girl.

Herbert Matter with the Knoll "K" trademark he designed. As pictured in *Life* Magazine, March 2, 1953.

A whimsical Knoll Textiles ad designed by Herbert Matter.

Mies van der Rohe, Ludwig (1886-1969)

Ludwig Mies van der Rohe achieved legendary fame as a Modern architect/designer. Born in Germany, the son of a stonemason, he attended trade school and worked in the family business. Mies[28] was a draftsman before becoming apprenticed to furniture designer Bruno Paul in Berlin. He completed his first house in 1907, and the design was noticed by Peter Behrens, considered at that time to be Germany's premier architect. Mies worked in Behren's office (as did Le Corbusier and Walter Gropius) until starting his own practice in 1911. He joined the German army in 1914, serving until 1918. After the war, he reestablished his practice, and his fame as a modern architect grew.

Mies would serve as chairman and director of many professional organizations during the 1920s and 1930s. He is perhaps best known for having served as the last director of the Bauhaus school when it was located in Dessau, and also after it was moved to Berlin. The Nazis forced the closure of the school in 1933. Mies came to live in the United States in 1938; he headed the department of architecture at the Armour Institute, later known as the Illinois Institute of Technology, where he served until 1959.

Throughout this time, Mies was working as an architect/designer. Along with Lily Reich, he designed the "Velvet and Silk" cafe at the 1927 Weissenhof exhibition. The exhibition introduced the cantilevered, tubular steel MR chair. Mies secured a patent on this design, and the chair was produced by Joseph Muller until 1929, and by Thonet until the 1940s.

The International Exhibition in Barcelona, Spain followed in 1928-1929, with Mies as the director of the German Pavilion. This famous pavilion has since been rebuilt on its original location. The design is a Mies classic. Eight thin steel columns support the slab roof which defines the space. Slabs of glass and marble are non-loadbearing screens dividing the space without actually enclosing it. The furniture designed for the pavilion has come to epitomize classic Modern design. The Barcelona

Tugendhat Arm Chair designed by Mies van der Rohe. Knoll produced this chair from 1965-1976.

Brno Chair manufactured by Knoll from 1961 to present.

chairs made their debut here, and were intended for the use of the King and Queen of Spain at the opening ceremony. They have a flat bar, steel construction. The upholstery was white kid leather. Matching ottomans for those waiting on the king and queen were also placed with the chairs. Mies would bring out a glass topped table the following year. Perhaps more than any other Modern furniture design, the Barcelona chair is instantly recognizable as a Modern classic.

Mies is also famous for the buildings and homes he designed. He extended his ideas from the Barcelona Exhibition for the Tugendhat family home in Brno, Czechoslovakia. Again we have glass walls, which can be retracted when desired to create open space. The Farnsworth House in Plano, Illinois also features glass exterior walls. Again, steel columns support ceilings. This "universal space" concept is found in Crown Hall, IIT's home for its department of architecture. Mies designed other buildings for the school as well. He designed the Seagram building in New York and the New National Gallery in Berlin, as well as other private homes.

Mies is known for what he did not build, as well. He envisioned our cities of glass and steel skyscrapers years before they were built.

Models and drawings of these skyscrapers have been found, along with drawings for furniture he surely meant for production. One of these designs, a tubular chaise, was built in 1977 for an exhibition of Mies furniture at the Museum of Modern Art in New York.

In 1948, Knoll secured the rights from Mies to produce the Barcelona chair. They were so successful that Florence Knoll commented that "they almost became a cliché of every new entrance lobby."[29] Over the years Knoll has added other Mies designs including the Brno chair and the Tugendhat chair.

Nakashima, George (1905-1990)

"A new type of man must be born who is as capable with machinery and tools as he is with a pencil..." said George Nakashima.[30] Trained as an architect, with degrees from MIT and the University of Washington, Nakashima brought together the arts of woodworking, furniture design, and manufacture.

Nakashima was first exposed to hands-on building, not only drawing, in 1934 while working in India for American architect Antonin Raymond. Acting as a construction superintendent on a dormitory, Nakashima trained the local labor force and devised construction methods. He then went to work in Raymonds' Tokyo office and while there studied Japanese carpentry. In Tokyo, he met his future wife, Marion. She was from Seattle and was teaching English in Tokyo.

He returned to the United States and took a tour of the West Coast to view famous buildings. Nakashima was dismayed by their construction. "They were badly, ignorantly built," he said. "The architects were over-specialized and knew nothing about building, like cooks who draw pictures of cakes but cannot make the batter themselves."[31] Looking for a design and construction process he could control entirely, he turned to furniture.

In 1942, Nakashima, his wife, and infant daughter were interned at an "evacuation camp" in Idaho because they were of Japanese ancestry. There, he gained most of his knowledge of woodworking from an elderly Japanese carpenter. In 1943, Antonin Raymond arranged for his release by offering him a job in Pennsylvania.

Nakashima made his home there, in the small town of New Hope. He continued to perfect his craft, not only in furniture design, but as an architect. He built his home and workshop there. The 800 square foot house which also acted as a showroom for clients was constructed of native woods, stone, and army surplus asbestos panels. The floors were wide, oiled walnut planks. There were an abundance of windows and most had a Japanese sliding panel in front of them, of wood framed paper. These "shojis" when closed provided insulation and privacy.

The Nakashima's living room was sometimes used as a showroom. As pictured in *House & Home*, March, 1952.

Aside from his work for Knoll (1946-1955) and his Origins Collection by Widdicomb (1958-1959), most of Nakashima's furniture was custom work done for individual clients. He preferred to use local woods such as walnut, birch, ash and cherry. He assembled the pieces by hand and would sometimes leave the knots or natural edges of the wood thereby turning imperfections into beauty marks. He did use machinery, but would hand finish the pieces himself to bring out the beauty of the wood. His tools were a combination of ancient Japanese saws, chisels, and modern power tools. Nakashima did not used varnishes, preferring wax or oils.

He strove for the integrity a master craftsman can bring to his work. "Hours spent by the true craftsman in bringing out the grain, which has long been imprisoned in the trunk of the tree, is an act of creation itself..." said George Nakashima.[32] He was a "true craftsman."

Nordstrom, Kurt
Nordstrom designed the No.145 Side Chair, which had a teak molded plywood seat and back on metal legs with wooden tips.

A sofa from Widdicomb's Origins Collection designed by George Nakashima.

Noguchi, Isamu (1904-1988)

Sculptor is probably the word most used to describe Isamu Noguchi, and yet this master sculptor is also known for his furniture and lighting designs. Noguchi was born in Los Angeles, but lived in Japan from the time he was two until he was thirteen. After attending a progressive school in New York, he became a premed student and took night classes in sculpting. After quitting college, he rented a studio, doing portrait busts. He obtained a Guggenheim Fellowship and traveled to Paris, where he spent several months in Brancusi's studio. Brancusi spoke no English and Noguchi spoke no French, the medium of communication was their art.

Noguchi began doing abstract sculpture, he wanted his art to have a message and be socially relevant. His abstracts did not sell, and he returned to doing portrait busts to support himself. He sculpted a bust of Martha Graham, whom he would work with for the next thirty years, designing stage sets for her. He also became a lifelong friend of Buckminster Fuller. The two did a show together, Noguchi's heads shown with Fuller's aluminum house.

In 1939, he received a commission from the president of the Museum of Modern Art, A. Congers Goodyear. For Goodyear's home, Noguchi designed a glass-topped coffee table with a sculptural base. This table was the forerunner of his classic 1947 coffee table, produced by Herman Miller. He also designed (for Herman Miller) a sofa and ottoman (1946), "rudder" dining table, coffee table, and a stool in 1949.[33] In 1954, Noguchi designed a rocking stool which Knoll produced. At Hans Knolls request, Noguchi modified the design for use as a table.

Being a sculptor, he came up with the idea of lighting sculpture from within. Noguchi called these pieces he did *lunars*. Noguchi then began experimenting with lamps having plastic and paper shades. One of these lamps caught the attention of Hans Knoll who agreed to manufacture a small version.

Noguchi traveled to Gifu, Japan in 1951, and saw a validation of his ideas in the ceremonial paper chochin lanterns produced there. He began designing lamps he called akari, meaning "light" in Japanese. The chochin used candlelight and were for ceremonial use, Noguchi's akari were electric and intended for everyday use. Like the chochin, they had paper shades that were collapsible. They had a beautiful simplicity and airy lightness, defying the heavy based table lamps then in use.

Noguchi continually came up with new forms for the shades, in part to defeat the imitations which cropped up almost immediately. He designed ever more intricate shapes, working with them for twenty-five years. In 1969, he designed a line of 30 akari which were signed, and sold as limited editions. A subsidiary of the Isamu Noguchi Foundation, Akari Associates, was formed and managed the line worldwide.

Noguchi was interested in landscape sculpture, aware that in sculpting public spaces he could create an environment that everyone could enjoy. He said that "...sculpture had to be an important part of the living experience and not just something for collectors to buy."[34] He would develop this "sculpting of space" into an art form. Noguchi integrated the elements of air, stone, and water. He designed stone parks with water flowing through them, fountains, dry stone gardens, and massive plazas. His works include the white marble garden he did for Yale University, a courtyard for Unesco, a water garden for Chase Manhattan, and a sculpture garden in Jerusalem. For the Hiroshima Peace Park, he designed two access bridges.

Noguchi produced individual sculptures as well, often working with massive pieces of stone. He could sculpt tons of stone into a highly polished perfect circle, or smooth, multi-colored segments, or into whimsical shapes. Some of these pieces can be seen at his museum, the Isamu Noguchi Garden Museum in Long Island City. Noguchi also had a working studio in Japan, which he carved from a hillside behind his home there. "Black Sun" is a famous piece completed prior to his death at age 84.

Rapson, Ralph (1914-)

A Michigan native, born in 1914, Ralph Rapson studied architecture at Cranbrook where he was friends with Charles Eames and Eero Saarinen. It was also at Cranbrook that he first met Florence Schust. In 1944 he was invited by Hans Knoll to join the Knoll Planning Unit to work on a project called "Equipment for Living." While there Rapson worked on a line of metal furniture as well as numerous designs for metal, molded plastic or fiberglass chairs but none were mass produced. Knoll did produce the "Rapson Line", a group of twelve pieces of wood and upholstered furniture. One of the pieces was a modern rocker, a rarity at that time. The line was produced in 1945 and 1946; it sold well and won critical praise. Rapson left Knoll in late 1945.

Several years later Hans Knoll helped Rapson secure a then important commission for the design of several new U.S. Embassy buildings with the stipulation that Knoll furniture would be specified.

Rapson taught at both the Illinois Institute of Technology (IIT) and MIT while practicing as a full-time architect. During his tenure at IIT from 1942 to 1946 Rapson collaborated with Laszlo Moholy-Nagy on interiors for B&O Railroad passenger cars. While at MIT during the early 1950s Rapson and his wife owned a modern design shop, Rapson, Inc. where they promoted the modern design esthetic. The shop contained furniture, textiles, ceramics, and metalwork, including Rapsons own lamp and furniture designs. He was the head of the Department of Architecture at the University of Minnesota from 1954 to 1984. Among Rapsons award winning architectural commissions are the Performing Arts Center at the University of California, Santa Cruz and the Cedar-Riverside urban planning project in Minneapolis Minnesota.[35]

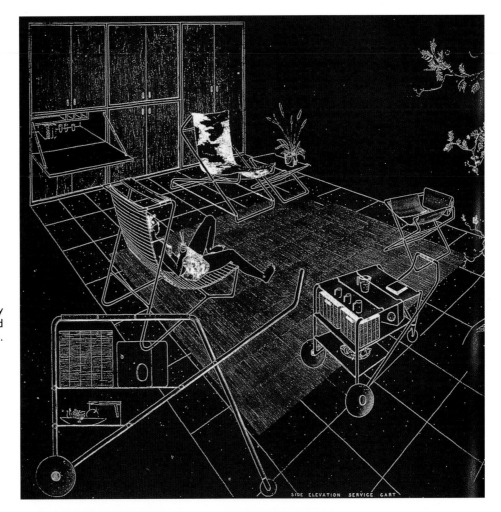

Outdoor metal furniture designs by Ralph Rapson for Knoll. As pictured in *Interiors* Magazine March 1946.

Risom, Jens (1916-)

Jens Risom was born in Copenhagen. His father was an architect who worked at home so Risom was exposed to design ideas from an early age. In 1938 Risom graduated from the school of Arts and Crafts in Copenhagen where he studied interior design and furniture.

He came to the United States in 1939 with an interest in modern design. He found little in the way of modern furniture manufacture, but decided to stay anyway. He worked briefly for Dan Cooper, a textile designer. He also designed furniture for an exhibition at the Rockefeller Home Center called "Collier's House of Ideas" in 1940. This exhibition brought him to the attention of architects, interior designers, and others interested in modern design.

Risom met Hans Knoll and the two traveled around the country looking for markets for modern furniture. By 1942, Hans was in business and Jens Risom designed Knolls' first line of modern furniture, on a free-lance basis. Risom then served in World War II as a member of the United States Army until 1945.

In Knoll Design, Risom says that when he came back in 1945 Hans wished to return to the arrangement they had before the war, however, it was apparent to Risom that this arrangement would no longer work. Florence Schust was now a part of Knoll, and in her Hans had found his "design intelligence."[36]

By 1946, Jens Risom had established his own firm, Jens Risom Design, Inc. He asked Knoll not to use his name in advertising as he did not wish to compete against his own designs. He was, and would continue to be, the sole designer for his firm. He controlled the design and manufacture of his product, and would become known for the quality of both.

His furniture line was not known for radical new designs but for a natural progression from year to year. He became known for his Scandinavian Modern designs. His business increased steadily, and he went from small manufacturing shops in New York to a manufacturing plant in Connecticut. The upholstery and final finishing was always done by hand, the quality of every detail was important to Risom and overseen by him.

As a designer, and as a craftsman, Risom strove for excellence. He remained true to wood at a time when modern designers were experimenting with plastics and metals. While he could appreciate the beauty of a plastic or metal chair, he wanted beauty and comfort in his own designs. He gave careful consideration to the use of the furniture, and the design of the human body, before designing it. He worked primarily in walnut or cherry, woods that have a richness of color and texture. "People need wood," he said.[37]

Saarinen, Eero (1910-1961)

Saarinen's father, Eliel, was a noted architect and designer who was one of the principal instructors at the Cranbrook Academy. Along with his father and mother, Saarinen designed furniture for the girls school, Kingswood, circa 1929.

Saarinen's mother, Loja, was a sculptor and Saarinen studied sculpture in Paris and architecture at Yale University, com-

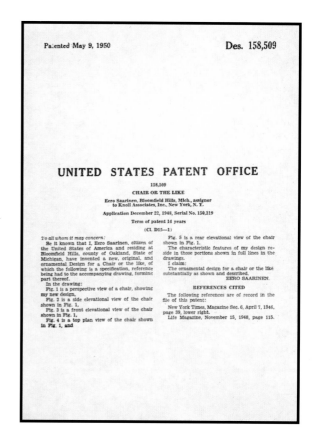

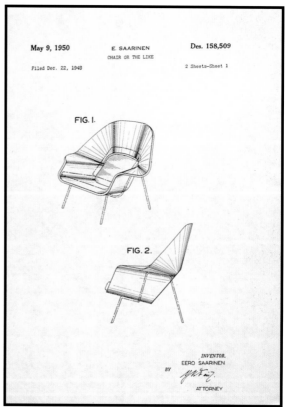

Eero Saarinen received a patent on the womb chair design May 9, 1950.

pleting his studies in 1934. He then worked with Norman Bel Geddes designing furniture. He joined his fathers architectural practice in Ann Arbor, Michigan, and became a partner in the firm Saarinen, Swanson, and Saarinen. This firm won a competition for the design of a Smithsonian Gallery of Art, circa 1939, which was never built.

In 1948, Saarinen won the competition for the design of the Jefferson Westward Expansion Memorial in St. Louis, Missouri. The Gateway Arch, as it is now known, established Saarinen as a world renowned architect. He designed MIT's Kresge auditorium, the General Motors Technical Center, and the TWA terminal at Kennedy Airport in New York. The CBS tower, John Deere office building in Moline, Illinois, and the main building for the Dulles International Airport were all designed by him, but completed after his death.

With Charles Eames, Saarinen won two first prizes in a competition sponsored by the Museum of Modern Art (1940) called "Organic Design in Home Furnishings." The judges included Alvar Aalto and Marcel Breuer. The winning designs had curved plywood forms that had been designed to accommodate the human form. They were hailed as "innovative", "creative", and even "revolutionary." They created a great deal of interest, and were featured in design magazines in the United States and overseas.

Saarinen's furniture designs for Knoll would include the classic Grasshopper chair and Womb chair, both designed in 1946. The Grasshopper chair was laminated wood, postwar shortages still making other materials hard to get. It was an extension of the work in bending plywood Saarinen had done with Eames. The Womb chair was a study in comfort, with its molded fiberglass, foam covered shell and ample dimensions. A person could curl up in it (the origin of the Womb chair thus explained) and turn around in it quite easily. Saarinen himself felt that the chair should stand on its own, as a piece of sculpture would, and yet be an attractive backdrop for the sitter.

Designed in 1946, the Womb chair took two years to produce. At that time, technological limitations dictated that fiberglass be used with a bonding agent. The resulting rough shell had to be covered in foam, and upholstered by necessity. Smooth fiberglass shells, like those used in Eames chairs, were not yet achievable. There were also concerns about the strength of the shell itself. These production problems were worked out, and the chair has been in continuous production by Knoll since the 1940s.

The pedestal chair and table were in response to Saarinen's dislike of furniture legs. "I wanted to clear up the slum of legs," he said.[38] Saarinen worked with Knoll's Donald Pettit on the shape of the chair, which Knoll began producing in the 1950s. Its flowerlike shape earned it the name "Tulip" chair, and it too became an instant classic. Due to its success, it was widely copied, but those copies simply do not have the perfection of the original Saarinen designs. Those perfect proportions were a tribute to his architectural background and early training as a sculptor.

Schultz, Richard (1930-)
Richard Schultz studied at the Illinois Institute of Technology in Chicago and Columbia University in New York. He joined Knoll in 1951 as a member of the Design Development Unit where one of his first assignments was assisting Harry Bertoia with work on Bertoia's wire furniture.

The Petal tables designed by Schultz were introduced in 1960 and received an award from Industrial Design Magazine. His steel wire chaise lounge was introduced the following year. In 1966 the Schultz Leisure Collection was introduced and received the American Institute of Interior Designers Award. Knoll produced the Pedal table until 1975 and the Leisure collection until 1988.

In 1986 Schultz designed the Lauren chair for Cadsana, Cadwallader, and Sangiorgio Associates. He has designed a group of garden furniture called Topiary which is reminiscent of shrubs trimmed into furniture shapes. Schultz has also reissued the Pedal tables and Leisure Collection which is now called the 1966 Collection. These pieces are being produced in his own shop in Pennsylvania.

Sorenson, Abel

A native of Denmark, Sorenson arrived in the United States in 1938. He became one of the early designers in Knoll's Planning Unit. By 1950, Knoll had produced several of his designs.

His double tray table for Knoll shows his creativity. It featured a webbed top on wooden legs and came with two Bentwood serving trays. These trays could rest on the webbing or be used individually. The double tray table came in a single tray version as well. He also designed a set of nesting tables with iron legs and bentwood tops.

Richard Stein Product Design Associates

Designed the No.700 Day Bed.

Tapiovaara, Ilmari (1914-

A Finnish designer, Tapiovaara studied industrial and interior design before working with Alvar Aalto and Le Corbusier during the 1930s. Tapiovaara was a pioneer in the design of "knock down" furniture. He concerned himself with the mass manufacture of furniture that could be stacked or folded for storage or economical shipment.

In 1948, he exhibited a chair in competition at the Museum of Modern Art in New York. He won gold medals for the designs he entered in the Milan Triennale exhibitions. These award winning designs included the "Lukki" and the "Kiki", both metal frame chairs with upholstered seat and back. Tapiovaara won many other awards as well. He designed for a number of companies including Thonet, Hackman, Merivaara, and Schauman. He also taught in Europe and the United States.

Tapiovaara's many interests led him to design in many other fields. He designed toys, radios, cutlery, and glassware. He painted and executed tapestries. He also did interior design work. Tapiovaara said, "Being a designer is rather like being a doctor; once you have the professional skill, you can practice anywhere you like. If what you do is good, it's good everywhere."[39] His major interior design credits include the Leningrad Concert Hall, the Intercontinental Hotel in Helsinki, airplane interiors for Finnair, as well as offices and theaters. Tapiovaara's stacking chair for Knoll was produced from 1947 to 1962.

END NOTES

[1]Quote is from Florence Knoll Bassett, when informed that a book was being written about Knoll. This quote, in another form, is also found in "Museum Watch," Echoes, 7(Winter,1998),34.

[2]Warren,Virginia Lee. "Woman Who Led an Office Revolution Rules an Empire." The New York Times. 1 September 1964, p.40.

[3]Quote from Florence Knoll, from the book Knoll Design : Eric Larrabee and Massimo Vignelli, Knoll Design . New York: Harry N. Abrams, 1981, 76.

[4]Larrabee, Eric and Massimo Vignelli, Knoll Design. New York: Harry N. Abrams, 1981, 42.

[5]Warren,Virginia Lee. "Woman Who Led an Office Revolution Rules an Empire." The New York Times. 1 September 1964, p.40.

[6]Newspaper and magazine articles, among other sources, give the date of the Knolls' marriage as 1944,1946, and 1948 respectively. The same range of dates has

been applied to the formation of Knoll Associates. The 1946 date is used by Knoll, and is the date most commonly found in our research.

[7]Larrabee, Eric and Massimo Vignelli, Knoll Design. New York: Harry N. Abrams, 1981, 22.

[8]Candee, Marjorie Dent, ed. Current Biography (Yearbook 1955). New York: The H. H. Wilson Company, 1955.

[9]Warren, Virginia Lee. "Woman Who Led an Office Revolution Rules an Empire." The New York Times. 1 September 1964, p.41.

[10]Larrabee, Eric and Massimo Vignelli, Knoll Design. New York: Harry N. Abrams, 1981, 22.

[11]Candee, Marjorie Dent, ed. Current Biography (Yearbook 1955). New York: The H. H. Wilson Company, 1955.

[12]Larrabee, Eric and Massimo Vignelli, Knoll Design. New York: Harry N. Abrams, 1981, 20.

[13]Peter M. Bode, Nick Jordan and Mel Silver, Knoll 50 Years of Design. West Germany: AWS/WWS YY-B50Y, 1987. Knoll 50 Years of Design is a full color, oversized publication, printed in West Germany by Knoll International in commemoration of its 50th anniversary.

[14]Gueft, Olga. "Knoll Associates move into the big time," Interiors, CX (May 1951), 75. The preface to this quote is that among "a few of the ultra sophisticated commentators in the field," there had been those closely examining the company for "some sign of monotony" to show that Knoll was "a little passe."

[15]Gueft, Olga. "Florence Knoll and the avant garde," Interiors, CXVI (July 1957), 60. We are given a glimpse of Florence's office here. Models (like the ones described as sitting on her windowsill) were used in solving design problems; sometimes larger versions of the same model would be built as the design was being worked out.

[16]Larrabee, Eric and Massimo Vignelli, Knoll Design. New York: Harry N. Abrams, 1981, 176. The preface to this quote explains that Hans seized an opportunity to use "blocked funds"; these were funds that had been set aside for use in post war European Countries. It is stated that a decision had been made by the State Department to use the funds on housing for U.S. Information Service personnel. Knoll worked with a "prefabricated house builder," supplying the furniture for those homes.

[17]Rae, Christine. Knoll au Louvre. New York: Chanticleer Press, 1971. Eero Saarinens full quotation can be found here.

[18]Larrabee, Eric and Massimo Vignelli, Knoll Design. New York: Harry N. Abrams, 1981, 146.

[19]Larrabee, Eric and Massimo Vignelli, Knoll Design. New York: Harry N. Abrams, 1981, 259.

[20]Richard Schultz, from the book Knoll Design: Eric larrabee and Massimo Vignelli, Knoll Design. New York: Harry N. Abrams, 1981, p.22.

[21]Rae, Christine. Knoll au Louvre. New York: Chanticleer Press, 1971.

[22]Larrabee, Eric and Massimo Vignelli, Knoll Design. New York: Harry N. Abrams, 1981, p.142.

[23]Larrabee, Eric and Massimo Vignelli, Knoll Design. New York: Harry N. Abrams, 1981, p.142.

[24]Larrabee, Eric and Massimo Vignelli, Knoll Design. New York: Harry N. Abrams, 1981, p.77.

[25]Warren, Virginia Lee. "Woman Who Led an Office Revolution Rules an Empire." The New York Times. 1 September 1964, p. 40.

[26]Warren, Virginia Lee. "Woman Who Led an Office Revolution Rules an Empire." The New York Times. 1 September 1964, p. 40.

[27]Eidelberg, Martin. Design 1935-1965 What Modern Was. New York: Harry N. Abrams, Inc., 1991.,62-63.

[28]Ludgwig Mies van der Rohe has been written about so many times, and is such a legendary figure, that it has become generally accepted to refer to him as simply "Mies" after the introductory use of his full name.

[29]Larrabee, Eric and Massimo Vignelli, Knoll Design. New York: Harry N. Abrams, 1981, p.36.

[30] "George Nakashima His Furniture His House His Way of Life" House and Home, (March, 1952), 80-89.

[31]"George Nakashima His Furniture His House His Way of Life" House and Home, (March, 1952), 80-89.

[32]"George Nakashima His Furniture His House His Way of Life" House and Home, (March, 1952), 80-89.

[33] The "rudder" table got its name from the shape of the leg upon which it rests, it is also called the "parabolic" table.

[34]The National Endowment for the Arts sponsored a series titled "American Masters" on public television. Noguchi was one of the artists featured in this series, in a segment which tells the story of his life and work. It was filmed after his death, and uses archival footage, still photographs, video of his works, and personal interviews to tell his story. Noguchi's quote comes from this video.

[35]Olivarez, Jennifer Komar. "Ralph Rapson and Hans Knoll," Echoes, 7 (Summer, 1998), 48-51 & 74-75.

[36]Larrabee, Eric and Massimo Vignelli, Knoll Design. New York: Harry N. Abrams, 1981, pg 46.

[37]Anderson, John. "The continuities of Jens Risom," Interiors, CXIX (October, 1959), 150-155, 220-222.

[38]Eidelberg, Martin. Design 1935-1965 What Modern Was. New York: Harry N. Abrams, Inc., 1991. p. 225. This section of the book talks about Eero Saarinen and his pedestal chair. Saarinen had to use metal for the chair's support, although he had designed it to be made of one component, plastic. He is quoted in the book as saying he will "look forward to the day" when plastics have evolved to the point where the chair can be made as he designed it.

[39]Morgan, Lee Ann. Contemporary Designers. U.S.A: MacMillan Publishers LTD., 1984., p.582.

This guide covers furniture manufactured or marketed by Knoll from 1941 through 1960. We have worked to make it as complete as possible, however, there are pieces for which only limited information was available.

We have found pieces from the early 1940s for which we have only general descriptions and little else. The book *Knoll Design* describes the first Knoll catalog from April 1942 as follows:

> ...a set of twenty-five pieces of grey cardboard with photographs pasted to them, enclosed (with a price list) in a brown folder. Fifteen of the pieces—the so-called "600" line —are Risom designs, in cherry wood, which by then had become available: cabinets, chests of drawers, bookcases, tables and a few chairs. The remainder the "200" and "800" line—are strange to look at today with the labels "Hans Knoll Furniture" attached to them, since they are over-stuffed and clumsy, and the opposite of everything Knoll has come to represent; these were mainly the work of Ernest Schwadron, a friend of Han's family from Vienna.

Hans Knoll Furniture ad, as pictured in *Interiors* Magazine August 1942.

Another bit of information comes from a Hans Knoll Furniture advertisement which appeared in *Interiors* magazine (August 1942). The advertisement shows four pieces from a "cherry wood" line. Only the 600 cloud cocktail table is included in this guide as we found no further information on the other pieces illustrated.

The Knolls purchased designs from abroad which sometimes did not appear in the regular Knoll catalogs and price lists. A photo from *Interiors* magazine (March 1947) shows a Bruno Matthsson chair, two Fritz Hansen chairs, and a cocktail table of unknown origin. The caption reads in part, "Hans and Mrs. Knoll, the former

Swedish knock down furniture imported by Knoll and displayed at Carson, Pirie, Scott & Company, Chicago. As pictured in *Interiors* Magazine August 1947.

Fritz Hansen and Bruno Matthsson chairs imported by Knoll. As pictured in *Interiors* Magazine, March ,1947.

Florence Schust, returned from Sweden with a group of home furnishings which they have arranged into a delightful apartment...." Another photo from *Interiors* (August 1947) shows a Knoll display at Carson, Pirie, Scott & Co. in Chicago. The caption reads in part, "Coffee table by Bruno Matthsson; armchair by Fritz Hansen; other pieces by Elias Svedberg; all in birch.....The Knoll poles and shelves are between the living room and dining room, all Knoll furnished." The Bruno Matthsson and Fritz Hansen pieces pictured are not listed in any Knoll material available and consequently were not included in this guide.

Knoll continued to purchase designs into the 1950s including a lighting collection from Italy. There are very possibly other pieces that Knoll marketed for a short time of which we are not aware.

We are always interested in acquiring additional literature and information about Knoll.

Sources

Information is largely from Knoll catalogs, brochures, advertisements, and press releases. Non-company sources were used but the most weight is given to Knoll material.

Dates

The production dates shown are documented dates when available. There were date gaps in the research materials and a number of Knoll catalogs, price lists, and brochures are undated. The material was viewed as a whole and the dates were derived from the information available.

Designer attribution

Knoll has always been proud of its designers and generous with attributions in company literature. However, Knoll did not always list a designer for each piece. Jens Risom requested in 1946 that Knoll not use his name in advertising and his designs are not attributed after this date. Some pieces are documented by Knoll to be by a specific designer while other similar pieces are not attributed. For example, a 1948 catalog lists Florence Knoll as the designer of desks,#15, #16, and #18, but offers no attribution for the very similar desks #13, #14, and #17. Also, attribution is somewhat ambiguous between Florence Knoll and The Planning Unit. We have listed those items as documented. In a very few instances we have placed a question mark after the designers name if the evidence strongly suggested them but no specific attribution was found.

Construction and materials

Knoll used a variety of woods over the years. During the war years cherry, cedar, and beech were used, but generally birch was favored in the 1940s. Clear maple was used in the early to middle 1950s, and walnut in the middle 1950s and beyond. Finishes were added or deleted as styles changed. Furniture with long production runs had some running changes as technologies advanced. For example, advances in production methods and materials allowed swivel chair bases to become lighter both in weight and appearance. Metal finishes over the years were offered in bright chrome, polished chrome, brushed chrome, nickel, painted lacquer,enamel, and fused plastic.

Advertisement from *Interiors* Magazine, November, 1952.

The following code numbers or letters were used in Knoll model numbers:

ABC-nesting tables	PS-plastic back
AC-arm chair	R-redwood top
BC-brushed chrome	RW-rosewood
C-caned doors	S-redwood slat top
C-chrome	S-swivel
E-ebony or ebonized	SC-side chair
F-1-black plastic laminate top	T-wood or teak
F-2-white plastic laminate top	U-upholstered
GP-grey plastic top	ULB-upholstered back
H-highback	U1/2- Upholstered separate seat and back
L-leather	W-webbed
M-white Italian marble with grey vein	W-wood or walnut
MC-Italian Cremo marble	WR-walnut plastic laminate
MW-wallen grey marble	WS-walnut swivel
N-Nakashima	W-solid walnut
NK- Nordiska Kompaniet	WV-walnut veneer
PC-polished chrome	W1-hanging cabinet
Plastic top-Plastic laminate over wood top.	1/2-half black and half white
PLB-plastic back	

Side Chair
666 W 1941-1961, 1998-
Jens Risom
W17.5", D21", H30.5". Cedar early production and later birch, beech, and walnut. Webbed seat and back. *Photo Courtesy of the Knoll Museum.*

Side Chair
666 W 1941-1961, 1998-
Jens Risom
(Top) W17.5", D21", H30.5". Cedar early production and later birch, beech, and walnut. Webbed seat and back

Side Chair
666 WSP 1941-1961, 1998-
Jens Risom
(Lower left) W17.5", D21", H30.5". Natural birch, beech or walnut. Wood back and webbed seat.

Side Chair
666 USP 1941-1961
Jens Risom
(Center right) W17.5", D21", H30.5". Natural birch, beech or walnut. Upholstered seat and back.

Arm Chair
666 UAC 1946?
Jens Risom
(Not shown) W ?", D21", H30.5". Natural birch, beech or walnut. Separate upholstered seat and back. Rare armed version of 666 side chair.

Side Chair
666 U 1941-1961
Jens Risom
W17.5", D21", H30.5". Natural birch, beech or walnut. Wood back and upholstered seat.

Arm Chair
652 U1/2 1941-1960
Jens Risom
(Lower left) W24", D28", H33". Clear birch frame, separate upholstered seat and back.

Chair 654 U 1941-1960
Jens Risom
(Lower right) W20", D28", H30". Natural birch frame, full upholstered seat and back.

Chair
654 U 1/2 1941-1960
Jens Risom
(Upper right) W20", D28", H30". Natural birch frame, separate upholstered seat and back.

Arm Chair
652 W 1941-1960
Jens Risom
(Upper left) W24", D28", H33". Clear birch or hard maple frame, webbed seat and back. Parachute straps were first used due to the many restrictions on materials during WWII.

Arm Chair
652 U 1941-1960
Jens Risom
W24", D28", H33". Clear birch or hard maple
frame, full upholstered seat and back.

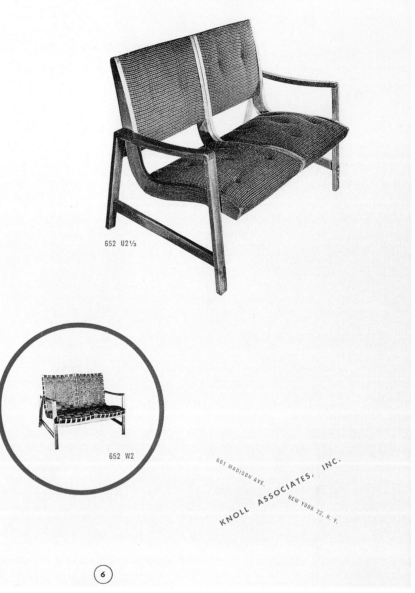

652 U2½

652 W2

601 MADISON AVE.

KNOLL ASSOCIATES, INC.

NEW YORK 22, N. Y.

(6)

Chair
654 W 1941-1960, 1998
Jens Risom
(Not shown) W20", D28", H30". Natural birch
frame, webbed seat and back. Webbing was war
surplus when introduced in 1941.

Chair
654 L 1941-1960
Jens Risom
W20", D28", H30". Natural birch frame, leather
webbed seat and back.

Settee
652 U2-1/2 1941-1948
Jens Risom
W44", D28", H33". Clear birch or hard maple frame,
separate upholstered seat and back.

Settee
652 W2 1941-1948
Jens Risom
(Lower left) W44", D28", H33". Clear birch or hard
maple frame, webbed seat and back.

Child's High Chair 1941-?
Jens Risom
W14", D26", H32". Spruce frame with canvas
webbing. *Photo Courtesy of the Knoll Museum.*

High Back Lounge Chair
655 UH 1945-1946
Ralph Rapson
Dimensions unknown. Birch frame with fully upholstered seat and back.
Photo courtesy of Ralph Rapson.

Lounge Chair
655 U 1945-1946
Ralph Rapson
Dimensions unknown. Birch frame
with fully upholstered seat and back.
Photo courtesy of Ralph Rapson.

Rocking Chair
657 U 1945-1946
Ralph Rapson
Dimensions unknown. Birch frame with fully upholstered seat and back. *Photo courtesy of Ralph Rapson.*

Lounge Chair
655 W 1945-1946
Ralph Rapson
Dimensions unknown. Birch frame
with webbed seat and back.

Rocking Chair
657 W 1945-1946
Ralph Rapson
Dimensions unknown. Birch frame
with webbed seat and back.

Sectional Sofa
658 U 1945-1946
Ralph Rapson
Dimensions unknown. Birch frame with fully
upholstered seat and back. Available as armless,
left or right armed section.
Also shown: 657 U Rocking Chair

High Back Rocking Chair
657 UH 1945-1946
Ralph Rapson
Dimensions unknown. Birch frame
with upholstered seat and back.

Settee
655 U2 1945-1946
Ralph Rapson
Dimensions unknown. Birch frame with fully
upholstered seat and back.

Lounge Chair
658 W 1945-1946
Ralph Rapson
Dimensions unknown. Birch frame
with webbed seat and back.

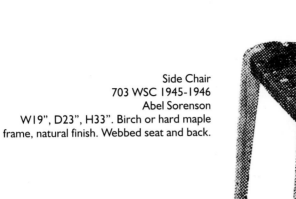

Side Chair
703 WSC 1945-1946
Abel Sorenson
W19", D23", H33". Birch or hard maple
frame, natural finish. Webbed seat and back.

Arm Chair
703 UAC 1945-1946
Abel Sorenson
W23", D23", H33". Birch or hard maple frame,
natural finish. Upholstered seat and back.

Side Chair with Arms
41 1946-1948
Abel Sorenson
W23.5", D24", H24". Solid wood frame with upholstered
seat and back. Also available with canvas webbing. *Photo
Courtesy of the Knoll Museum.*
Also shown: 15 Desk.

Arm Chair with Swivel Base
43 1946-1949
Florence Knoll
W26", D23.5", H30". Fully upholstered. Also
available with leather upholstery. Wood frame
in clear birch or hard maple in natural finish.

Side Chair
40 1946-1949
Abel Sorenson
W18.5", D24", H24". Solid wood frame,
upholstered seat and back.

Arm Chair
43 1946-1949
Florence Knoll
W26", D23.5", H30". Fully upholstered. Also
available with leather upholstery. Wood frame
in clear birch or hard maple in natural finish.

Work Chair
T60 1947-1950
Odelberg Olson
W17", D18", H31". Wood work
chair with wooden seat.

Work Chair
T60 U 1947-1950
Odelberg Olson
W17", D18", H31". Wood work
chair with upholstered seat.

Stacking Chair
130 1947-1966
Andre Dupre
W19.5", D21", H32". Tubular steel frame,
polished chrome or black finish. Black or white
vinyl cord seat and back. Andre Dupre was the
French manufacturer of Bertoia chairs.

Webbed Stool
667 W 1947?-1958, 1998
Jens Risom
W15", D16.5", H18". Spruce, birch, or maple
stool with webbed seat. This stool is attributed
to Jens Risom as part of the "600" series.
However a 1947 price list attributes it to
Florence Knoll.

Bar Stool
46 1947-1949
Henry Kann
W16", D19.5", H42". Clear
birch or hard maple with
natural finish.

Hardoy Chair
198 L 1947-1950
Bonet, Kurchan, and Hardoy
W31", D27.5", H34.5"". Leather sling seat on rod iron frame.
Also 198 with cloth sling. Also called the "Butterfly" o r "AA" chair.
Photo Courtesy of the Knoll Museum.

Stacking Chair
141 1947-1962
Ilmari Tapiovaara
W17.5", D21", H30". Clear birch and molded plywood finished clear,
walnut, or ebony. Upholstered seat, wood back. Also available as 140
with wood seat and back and 142 with upholstered seat and back.
Photo Courtesy of the Knoll Museum.

Chair
N19 1947-1955
George Nakashima
W24", D20", H28". Frame of clear birch with natural finish. Mortised and tenoned joints. Also available in walnut, cherry, or ebony. *Photo Courtesy of the Knoll Museum.*

Chair
N20 1950-1953
George Nakashima
W20", D21", H27.5". Frame of clear birch with natural finish. Mortised and tenoned joints. Also available in walnut, cherry, or ebony.

Side Chair
72 P*PSB 1948-1976
Eero Saarinen
W21.5", D20", H31.75". Plastic back available in a variety of
colors. Upholstered seat. Tubular steel legs, black finish,
available in other finishes. *Photo Courtesy of the Knoll Museum.*

Swivel Side Chair
72 PS-PC 1948-1975
Eero Saarinen
W21.5", D20", H30.5"-33.25".
Aluminum base, polished chrome
finish. Other finishes available.
Upholstered seat, plastic back
available in a variety of colors.

Swivel Side Chair
72 US*US-BC 1948-1998
Eero Saarinen
W21.5", D20", H30.5"-33.25".
Aluminum base, polished chrome
finish. Other finishes available.
Upholstered seat and back.

Side Chair
72 U*UPC 1948-1998
Eero Saarinen
W21.5", D20", H31.75". Chrome
plated tubular steel base, other
finishes available. Upholstered seat
and back.

Side Chair
72 PLB 1948-1975
Eero Saarinen
W21.5", D20", H31.75". Walnut or teak veneer legs, available in a variety of finishes. Plastic back available in a variety of colors. Upholstered seat.

Side Chair
72 ULB 1948-1976
Eero Saarinen
W22", D20", H32". Walnut or teak veneer legs, available in a variety of finishes. Seat and back upholstered. *Photo Courtesy of the Knoll Museum.*

Desk Chair
47 1949-1962
Franco Albini
W22", D23.25", H31". Steel rod base, available in a variety of finishes.
Also shown: 80 Desk.

Desk Chair
48 1949-1967
Franco Albini
W22", D23.25, H31". Birch, maple, or walnut
base, available in a variety of finishes.

Arm Chair
147 1950-1953
Joseph Frank
W19.5", D21", H33". Bent-ash construction with cane seat and back.
Manufactured by Thonet of Czechoslovakia. Also available with
removable foam rubber seat cushion.

Side Chair
146 1950-1953
Joseph Frank
W17", D21", H33". Bent-ash construction with cane seat and back.
Manufactured by Thonet of Czechoslovakia. Also available with
removable foam rubber seat cushion.

Upholstered Swivel Chair
44S 1950-1954
Designer unknown
(Upper left) W26", D26", H31.5". Swivel base, clear birch with natural, standard walnut, or ebony finish. Also available with top grain leather upholstery.

Upholstered Arm Chair
44 1950-1954
Designer unknown
(Lower right) W26", D26", H31.5". Legs, clear birch with natural, standard walnut, or ebony finish. Also available with top grain leather upholstery.

Upholstered Settee
45 1950
Designer unknown
W48", D26", H31.5". Legs, clear birch with natural, standard walnut, or ebony finish. Also available with top grain leather upholstery.

Stacking Stool
75 1950-1970
Florence Knoll
Diam. 13", H18". Birch wood top with bent rod iron legs with baked white enamel. Later production available with laminate top in black, white, or maple.
Photo Courtesy of the Knoll Museum.

Metal Chair
132 1950-1952
Donald Knorr
W20", D19.5", H29". Round steel legs. Sheet metal seat
and back. Also available as 132 U with fully upholstered
seat with rubber cushion. This chair shared first prize for
seating in the 1949 Museum of Modern Art Low-Cost
Design Competition. *Photo Courtesy of the Knoll Museum.*

Arm Chair
71 ULB 1952-1976
Eero Saarinen
W26", D24", H31.5". Walnut or teak veneer legs.
Available in a variety of finishes

Arm Chair
71 USB*UPC 1950-1998
Eero Saarinen
W26", D24", H31.5". Tubular steel chrome plated legs, other finishes available.

Swivel Arm Chair
71 WS 1952-1976
Eero Saarinen
W26", D24", H31.5"-34.25". Walnut swivel base, available in a variety of finishes.

Swivel Arm Chair
71 S 1950-1998
Eero Saarinen
W26", D24", H31.5"-34.25".
Aluminum base with brushed chrome finish, other finishes available.

Knoll International Inc.
745 Fifth Avenue, New York 10022

Bertoia

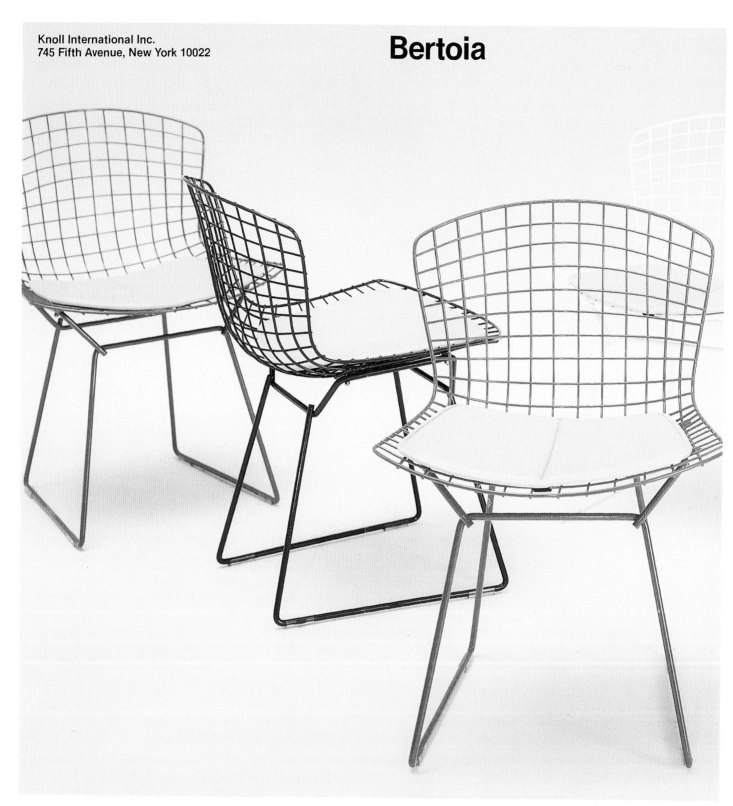

Side Chair
420 -2 1952-1998
Harry Bertoia
W21", D22.5", H30". Welded steel wire seat and back, available in white fused plastic or other finishes. Steel rod base available in white fused plastic or other finishes. Upholstered foam rubber, detachable seat pad.

Side Chair
420 -3 1954-1984
Harry Bertoia
W21", D22.5", H30". Welded steel wire seat and back, available in
white fused plastic or other finishes. Steel rod base available in
white fused plastic or other finishes. Separate seat and back foam
rubber covers

Side Chair
427 1956-1973
Harry Bertoia
W20.5", D22", H30.5". Plastic seat and back available in a variety
of colors. Steel rod base available in polished chrome or other
finishes. *Photo Courtesy of the Knoll Museum*.

Side Chair
420 -4 1952-1998
Harry Bertoia
W21", D22.5", H30". Welded
steel wire seat and back, available
in white fused plastic or other
finishes. Steel rod base available in
white fused plastic or other
finishes. Fully upholstered foam
rubber seat and back.
Also shown: 310 F Extension
Dining Table.

Child's Chair
425 1955-1981, 1983-1984
Harry Bertoia
(Left) W15.75", D16.25", H24".
Welded steel wire seat and back
available in polished chrome or
other finishes. Steel rod base
available in polished chrome or
other finishes. Upholstered foam
rubber detachable seat pad.

Child's Chair
426 1955-1975
Harry Bertoia
(Right) W13.25", D13.5", H20".
Welded steel wire seat and back
available in polished chrome or
other finishes. Steel rod base
available in polished chrome or
other finishes. Upholstered
foam rubber, detachable seat pad.
Also shown: 87 Noguchi Child's
Table.

Side Chair
145 1954-1960
Kurt Nordstrom
W17.25", D19.25", H30.5". Tubular steel frame, black finish with wood tips on legs. Seat and back molded teak plywood with natural finish.
Photo Courtesy of the Knoll Museum.

Bar Stool
428 1962-1973, 1983-1998
Harry Bertoia
W21", D22.5", H42.5". Nickel plated or black finish steel base .
Plastic shell available fully upholstered , or upholstered on the inside
only. Also available with with welded wire seat and back.

Secretarial Swivel Chair
76 S-PC 1953-1968
Eero Saarinen
W18.5", D18.5", H29.5"- 34.5". Aluminum
base polished chrome finish, other finishes
available.

Swivel Base Drafting Stool
77 S-BC 1956-1968
Eero Saarinen
W18", D20", H35.5"- 40.5". Aluminum
base brushed chrome finish, other
finishes available.

Pedestal Arm Chair
150 1956-1998
Eero Saarinen
W26". D23.5", H32". Aluminum base with fused plastic finish. Available in a variety of colors. Plastic shell matches base. Also available with revolving shell. Upholstered seat pad.
Also shown: 174F Pedestal Table.

Pedestal Side Chair
151 1956-1996
Eero Saarinen
W19.5", D22", H32". Aluminum base with fused plastic finish. Available in a variety of colors. Shell matches color of base. Also available with revolving shell. Upholstered seat pad.

Pedestal Arm Chair
150 U 1956-1998
Eero Saarinen
(Right) W26". D23.5", H32". Aluminum base with fused plastic finish. Available in a variety of colors. Plastic shell matches base. Plastic shell upholstered on inside only. Also available with revolving shell.

Pedestal Side Chair
151 U 1956-1998
Eero Saarinen
(Left) W19.5", D22", H32". Aluminum base with fused plastic finish. Available in a variety of colors. Plastic shell upholstered on inside. Shell matches color of base. Also available with revolving shell.

Swivel Side Chair
151 DS 1956-1998
Eero Saarinen
(Center) W19.5", D22", H32". Aluminum swivel with fused plastic finish. Available in a variety of colors. Upholstered seat pad. Shell matches color of base.

Swivel Side Chair
151 UDS 1956-1998
Eero Saarinen
(Right) W19.5", D22", H32". Aluminum swivel with fused plastic finish. Available in a variety of colors. Plastic shell upholstered on inside. Shell matches color of base.

Swivel Arm Chair
150 DS 1956-1998
Eero Saarinen
W26", D23.5", H32". Aluminum swivel with fused plastic finish. Available in a variety of colors. Shell matches color of base. Upholstered seat pad only. Also available as 150 UDS with plastic shell upholstered on inside only.

Pedestal Stool
152 S 1957-1984
Eero Saarinen
Diam.15", H16".
Foam rubber upholstered cushion on Aluminum base with fused plastic finish. Available in a variety of colors.

Rocking Stool
85 T 1955-1960
Isamu Noguchi
Diam. 14", H10.5". Solid teak or walnut with chrome plated wire.

Rocking Stool
86 T 1955-1960
Isamu Noguchi
Diam. 14", H16.75". Solid teak or walnut with chrome plated wire.
Photo Courtesy of the Knoll Museum.

Swivel Arm Chair
84 -BC 1956-1964
Florence Knoll
(Center) W26.75", W26.75", H33.25"-36"
Max. Aluminum base, brushed chrome finish,
other finishes available.

Swivel Arm Chair
84 WS 1956-1964
Florence Knoll
(Left) W26.75", W26.75", H33.25"-36" Max.
Walnut base, available in a variety of finishes.

Arm Chair
84 ULB 1956-1964
Florence Knoll
(Lower right) W26.75", D26.75", H32.5".
Walnut or teak veneer legs, available in a
variety of finishes.

Chair
21 1946-1967
Jens Risom
(Right) W23 ", D30.5", H30.5". Clear birch, natural
finish frame. Available in a variety of finishes. Also
available as 21 W with walnut frame.

Settee
22 1946-1962
Jens Risom
(Left) W49 ", D30.5", H30.5". Clear birch, natural
finish frame. Available in a variety of finishes. Also
available as 22 W with walnut frame.

Sofa
23 1946-1962
Jens Risom
W73", D30.5", H30.5". Clear birch, natural finish frame.
Available in a variety of finishes. Also available as 23 W with
walnut frame. Also shown: N10 Coffee Table.

Chair
35 1946-1953
Jens Risom
(Lower right) W29", D33.5", H31". Legs, clear birch or hard maple with
natural, standard walnut, or ebony finish.

Settee
38 1950-1953
Jens Risom
(Upper left) W54", D33.5", H31". Legs, clear birch or hard maple with natural,
standard walnut, or ebony finish.

Armless Chair
201 1947-1951
Elias Svedberg
(Left) W28.5", D30", H34". Solid wood legs in clear maple or
birch. Natural finish.
Also shown: Left to right. 127 Chest, 110 Coffee Table, 23 Sofa,
and 652U Armchair.

Sofa
37 1946-1953
Jens Risom
W78", D33.5", H31". Legs, clear birch or hard maple with natural, standard walnut, or ebony finish.

Settee
27 1949-1970
Florence Knoll
W63", D31", H30". Early production legs clear birch with natural finish, later production maple or walnut, available in a variety of finishes.

Chair
25 1947-1970
Florence Knoll
(Left) W30", D31", H30". Early production legs clear birch with natural finish, later production maple or walnut, available in a variety of finishes.

Sofa
26 1947-1970
Florence Knoll
(Right) W90", D31", H30". Early production legs clear birch with natural finish, later production maple or walnut, available in a variety of finishes. Also shown: N10 Table.

Arm Chair
25 BC 1949-1970
Florence Knoll
W30", D31", H30". Steel legs, brushed
chrome finish. Other finishes available.

Settee
27 BC 1949-1970
Florence Knoll
W63", D31", H30". Steel legs, brushed chrome finish. Other finishes available.

Sofa
26 BC 1949-1970
Florence Knoll
W90", D31", H30". Steel legs, brushed chrome finish. Other finishes
available.

Arm Chair "Grasshopper" Chair
61 U 1946-1965
Eero Saarinen
W23", D31", H29" . Birch or maple laminate base, available in a variety
of finishes. *Photo Courtesy of the Knoll Museum*.

Ottoman, "Grasshopper" Chair
62 1954-1964
Eero Saarinen W23.5", D17.75", H16". Birch or
maple laminate base, available in a variety of
finishes. Also shown: 61U Chair.

49 Lounge chair, wood

Lounge Chair
49 1949-1967
Franco Albini
W25", D28", H29.5". Birch, maple, or walnut base,
available in a variety of finishes.

"Scissor Chair"
92 1948-1966
Pierre Jeanneret
W23", D31", H29". Birch or maple wood
frame, available in a variety of finishes.
Photo Courtesy of the Knoll Museum.

Ottoman "Womb Chair Ottoman"
74 1950-1998
Eero Saarinen
(Lower left) W25.5", D20", H16". Steel rod base with polished
chrome, available in other finishes. Upholstered shell and seat cushion.

Lounge Chair "Womb Chair"
70 1948-1998
Eero Saarinen
(Right) W40", D34", H35.5". Steel rod base with polished chrome,
available in other finishes. Upholstered shell , upholstered seat and back
cushions.

Settee "Womb Settee"
73 1950-1978
Eero Saarinen(Upper left)
W62", D34", H35.5". Steel rod base with polished chrome, available in
other finishes. Upholstered shell, upholstered seat and back cushions.

Large Diamond Chair
422 1954-1979, 1987-1998
Harry Bertoia
W45", D32", H27.75". Welded steel wire seat and
back, available in polished chrome or other
finishes. Steel rod base available in polished chrome
or other finishes. Fully upholstered foam rubber,
detachable cover.

Small Diamond Chair
421 1952-1984, 1987-1998
Harry Bertoia
W33.75", D28", H30.5". Welded steel wire seat
and back available in polished chrome or other
finishes. Steel rod base available in polished
chrome or other finishes. Fully upholstered foam
rubber, detachable cover.

Opposite Page:

Diamond Chair Ottoman
424 1952-1984, 1987-1998
Harry Bertoia
W24", D17.25", H14.75". Steel wire seating unit, with
steel rod base. Removable seat pad. Available in polished
chrome or other finishes.

High Back Diamond "Bird Chair"
423 C 1952-1984, 1987-1998
Harry Bertoia
W38.5", D34.5", H39.25". Welded steel wire seat and
back, available in polished chrome or other finishes.
Steel rod base available in polished chrome or other
finishes. Fully upholstered foam rubber, detachable cover.
Also shown: 400 Bench, and 422 Large Diamond Chair.

Small Diamond Chair
421 -2 1952-1984, 1987-1998
Harry Bertoia
W33.75", D28", H30.5". Welded steel wire seat and
back available in in polished chrome or other finishes.
Steel rod base available in polished chrome or other
finishes. Upholstered foam rubber, detachable seat pad.

Chair
31 1954-1968
Florence Knoll
W24", D27", H29". Tubular steel base with black finish. Brushed
chrome or polished chrome finishes available.

Settee
32 1954-1968
Florence Knoll
W48", D27", H29". Tubular steel base with black finish. Brushed
chrome or polished chrome finishes available.
Also shown: 307 1/2 Coffee Table.

Above:
Sofa
96 -1 1953-1970
designer unknown
W80", D30", H29". Steel legs, black finish. Other finishes available.

Below:
Sofa
33 1954-1968
Florence Knoll
W72", D27", H29". Tubular steel base with black finish. Brushed chrome or polished chrome finishes available.

Arm Chair
95 -1 1953-1970
designer unknown
W29.5", D30", H29". Steel legs, black finish.
Other finishes available.

Settee
97 -1 1953-1970
designer unknown
W50.5", D30", H29". Steel legs, black finish.
Other finishes available.

Sofa
96 -2 1954-1970
designer unknown
W80", D30", H29". Square tapered maple legs
finished clear, walnut, or ebony.

Arm Chair
95 -2 1954-1970
designer unknown
W29.5", D30", H29". Square tapered
maple legs finished clear, walnut, or
ebony.

Settee
97 -2 1954-1970
designer unknown
W50.5", D30", H29". Square tapered maple legs finished
clear, walnut, or ebony.

Barcelona Chair
250 1948-1998
Ludwig Mies van der Rohe
W30", D30", H30". Frame stainless steel, polished finish.
Saddle leather straps. Cushions covered in leather with
individual button tufted panels.

Barcelona Stool
251 1954-1998
Ludwig Mies van der Rohe
W23", D22", H14 1/2". Frame stainless
steel, polished finish. Saddle leather straps.
Cushion covered in leather with individual
button tufted panels.

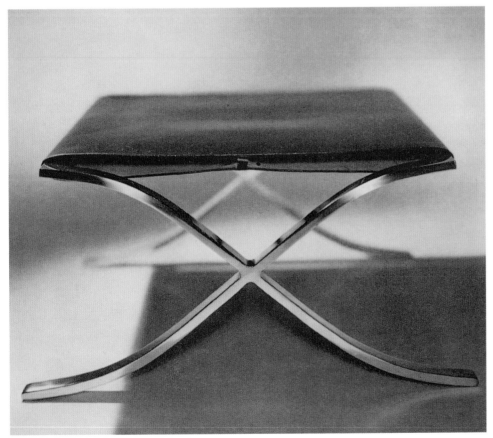

Barcelona Stool
253 1954-1978
Ludwig Mies van der Rohe
W23", D22", H12". Stainless steel base.
Natural saddle leather sling.

Lounge Chair
655 1955-1962
Lewis Butler
W25.5", D29", H29.5". Maple frame, seat and back is angled walnut panels. Later production 655 W has walnut frame, seat, and back.

Settee
656 1955
Lewis Butler
(Not shown) W46", D24.75", H29". Maple frame, seat and back is angled walnut panels.

Sofa
676 1955-1961
Lewis Butler
W80", D30", H28.25". Maple and walnut base and frame with natural webbing. Also shown: 358 Coffee Table.

Parallel Bar System Sofa
53 1955-1973
Florence Knoll
W84", D31", H30" . Steel base
with brushed chrome and black
finish. Other finishes available.

Parallel Bar System Lounge Chair
51 1955-1973
Florence Knoll
W24", D31", H30". Steel base with brushed
chrome and black finish. Other finishes
available.

Parallel Bar System Settee
52 1955-1973
Florence Knoll
W56", D31", H30". Steel base with
brushed chrome and black finish.
Other finishes available.

Parallel Bar System Sofa
57 1955-1973
Florence Knoll
W89", D31", H30". Steel base with brushed
chrome and black finish. Other finishes available.

Parallel Bar System Arm Chair
55 1955-1973
Florence Knoll
W29", D31", H30". Steel base with brushed chrome
and black finish. Other finishes available.

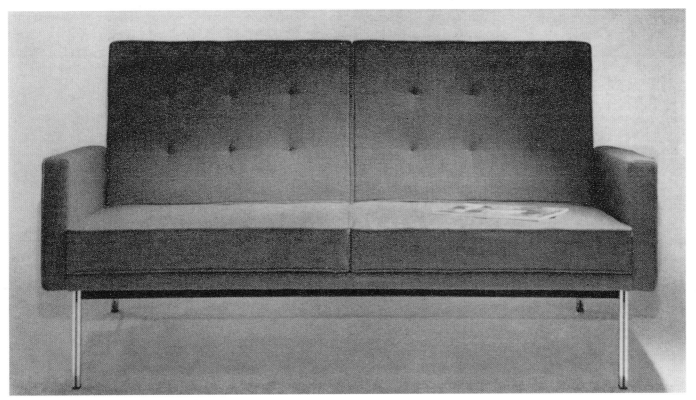

Parallel Bar System Settee
56 1955-1973
Florence Knoll
W61", D31", H30". Steel base with brushed chrome and black finish.
Other finishes available.

Sofa
53 W 1955-1973
Florence Knoll
W89", D31", H30". Walnut base available in a variety
of finishes. Also available as 53 T in teak.

Settee
52 W 1955-1973
Florence Knoll
W56", D31", H30". Walnut base available in a variety
of finishes. Also available as 52 T in teak.

Lounge Chair
51 W 1955-1973
Florence Knoll
W24", D31", H30". Walnut base available in a variety
of finishes. Also available as 51 T in teak.

Sofa
57 W 1955-1973
Florence Knoll
W89", D31", H30". Walnut base available in a
variety of finishes. Also available as 57 T in teak.

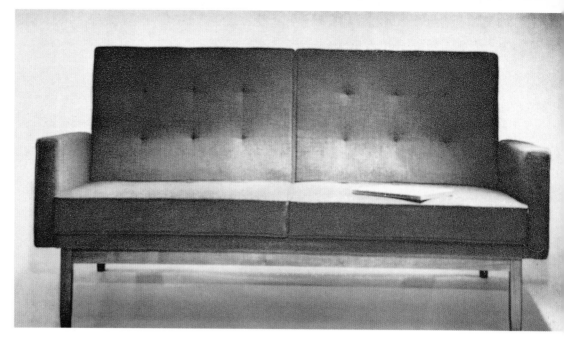

Settee
56 W 1955-1973
Florence Knoll
W61", D31", H30".
Walnut base available in a
variety of finishes. Also
available as 56 T in teak.

Sofa
578 1954-1970
Florence Knoll
(Not shown) W120", D28.5", H30". Square tubular steel base, black finish. Other finishes available. Same as 575 but sofa only. Also available as 2578BC with brushed chrome legs and 2578PC with polished chrome legs.

Sofa
575 1954-1970
Florence Knoll
W120", D28.5", H30". Square tubular base with black finish. Other finishes available. Walnut end case with drawers. Available in a variety of finishes. May be mounted right or left. Also available as 2575 with polished chrome legs.

Left:
Arm Chair
55 W 1955-1973
Florence Knoll
W29", D31", H30". Walnut base available in a variety of finishes. Also available as 55 T in teak.

Sofa
2577 BC 1954-1970
Florence Knoll
W120", D28.5", H30". Square tubular steel base, polished chrome finish. Other finishes available. Walnut open end case with glass top. Also available as 577 with black metal legs and 2577PC with polished chrome legs.

Sofa
576 1954-1970
Florence Knoll
W120", D28.5", H30". Square tubular steel base, black finish. Other finishes available. Walnut end case with magazine rack. Also available as 2576BC with brushed chrome legs and 2576PC with polished chrome legs.

Lounge Chair
2551 1955-1976
Florence Knoll
W24", D31", H30". Square tubular steel
base , brushed chrome finish. Other
finishes available.

Sofa
2553 1955-1976
Florence Knoll
W84", D31", H30". Square tubular steel base , brushed chrome finish.
Other finishes available.

Settee
2552 1955-1976
Florence Knoll
W56", D31", H30". Square tubular steel base ,
brushed chrome finish. Other finishes available.

Sofa
2557 1955-1976
Florence Knoll
W89", D31", H30". Square
tubular steel base , brushed
chrome finish. Other finishes
available.

Settee
2556 1955-1976
Florence Knoll
W61", D31", H30". Square tubular steel base ,
brushed chrome finish. Other finishes available.

Arm Chair
2555 1955-1976
Florence Knoll
W29", D31", H30". Square tubular steel base ,
brushed chrome finish. Other finishes available.

Sofa
67 1958-1975
Florence Knoll
W90", D30", H31.5". Square tubular
steel base, brushed chrome finish.
Other finishes available.

Settee
66 1958-1975
Florence Knoll
W56", D30", H31.5". Square tubular steel base,
brushed chrome finish. Other finishes available.

Lounge Chair
65 1958-1975
Florence Knoll
W28", D30", H31.5". Square tubular steel base,
brushed chrome finish. Other finishes available.

Sofa with Arms
67 A 1958-1973
Florence Knoll
W90", D30", H31.5". Square tubular steel base,
brushed chrome finish. Other finishes available.
Also shown: 2518RW Coffee Table, 2514MC End Table

Arm Chair
65 A 1958-1973
Florence Knoll
W34", D30", H31.5". Square tubular steel base,
brushed chrome finish. Other finishes available.

Tables

Cloud Cocktail Table
600 1945
Jens Risom
W40", D31", H18".

Side Table
625 L 1945
Jens Risom?
Diam. 25", H21".

Dining Table
632 D 1945
Jens Risom
W32", D32", H28.5".

Coffee Table
638 C 1945
Jens Risom
W38", D23", H18".

53

50

52

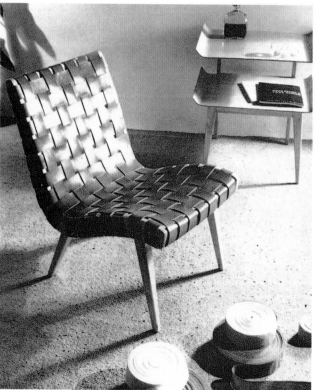

Above:
Double Tray Table
52 1946-1950
Abel Sorenson
(Lower right) W38.25", D19", H17.75". Wood frame with webbed top.
Two bentwood serving trays.

Table
53 1946-1949
Abel Sorenson
(Not shown) W24.5", D19", H18". Molded plywood top.

Single Tray Table
50 1946-1950
Abel Sorenson
(Left) W24.75", D19", H17.75". Wood frame with webbed top.
Bentwood serving tray. Tray or webbed stool available separately.

Left:
Two Tier Table
55 1946-1949
Abel Sorenson
W24.5", D21.5", H25". Molded plywood tops. Also shown: 654 Chair.

Extension Dining Table
NK 4 1947-1951
Elias Svedberg
W31.5" min. to 63" max., D31.5", H28.25". Elm with
natural finish, base and legs birch with natural finish.
Manufactured in Sweden by Nordiska Kompaniet.
Also shown: 666 USP chair.

Rectangular Wood Side Table
NK 5 1947-1951
Elias Svedberg
W26", D17.25", H20.75". Elm with
natural finish, base and legs birch with
natural finish. Manufactured in Sweden
by Nordiska Kompaniet.
Also shown: 201 Armless Chair.

Table
NK 6 1947-1951
Elias Svedberg
Diam. 26.25". H20.50". Elm with
natural finish, base and legs birch with
natural finish. Manufactured in Sweden
by Nordiska Kompaniet.

Dish Top Table
NK 9 1947-1950
Elias Svedberg
Diam. 35.5", H18". Elm with natural
finish, base and legs birch with natural
finish. Also available in burled birch
veneer with base and legs in natural
birch finish. Manufactured in Sweden by
Nordiska Kompaniet.

Table
NK 7 1947-1951
Elias Svedberg
Diam. 30", H20.50". Elm with natural
finish, base and legs birch with natural
finish. Manufactured in Sweden by
Nordiska Kompaniet.

Square Coffee Table
NK 8 1947-1950
Elias Svedberg
W30", D30", H19.75". Elm and birch with natural finish.
Manufactured in Sweden by Nordiska Kompaniet.

Coffee Table
100 1947-1950
Designer unknown
W34", D24", H18". Clear birch,
natural finish.

Nesting Tables
57 ABC 1950
Hosken design
W22", D16.75", H21.5"/ W20.5", D15", H19"/ W19",
D13.75", H16". Set of three tables.

Nesting Tables
56 ABC 1947-1950
Abel Sorenson
W24.5", D19", H19", 17", 15". Set of three tables of
decreasing size. Rod iron legs with bentwood tops.

Small Tripod Table
103 1947-1961
Hans Bellman
Diam. 24", H20". Demountable birch top with folding ebony
legs. Also available with white or walnut plastic top.

114 Large tripod table, Hans Bellman design

Large Tripod Table
114 1947-1954
Hans Bellman
Diam. 36", H22". Demountable
birch top with folding tripod base.
Also available with plastic top.

Dinette Table
102 1947-1949
Designer unknown
W32", D32", H28". Birch top and legs.
Also shown: 666W Chair.

Sofa Table
108 1948
Alexander Girard
W59", D17", H16". Birch wood natural
finish, black metal legs.

Extension Dining Table
301 1950-1956
Designer unknown
W60" min. to 78" max., D34", 28.5". Birch
plywood with natural finish. One 18" leaf.
Also available as 301W in walnut.
Also shown: 146 and 147 Chairs.

"Popsicle" Dining Table
302 1947-1956
Hans Bellman
Diam. 48", H28". Birch top with
three ebony finished legs. Also
available with plastic top in a variety
of finishes.
Also shown: 72UPC Chairs.

Coffee Table
110 1948-1954
Abel Sorenson
W59.75", D23.75", H17". Boat-shaped walnut top
with birch legs and natural finish.

Stacking Table
106 1948-1964
Florence Knoll
W32", D32", H29". Maple base. Clear lacquer, walnut,
or ebony finishes available. Black or white plastic top.
Available in other sizes and materials.

Coffee Table
N 10 1946-1954
George Nakashima
W38", D34", H16.5". Solid birch top with walnut sides and legs.
Available in natural, standard walnut, or ebony finish.

Table
N 11 1948-1949
George Nakashima
W20", D37", H15". Solid butternut top,
birch sides and legs.
Also shown: 700 Day Bed and Cartree.

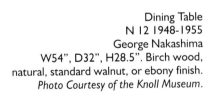

Dining Table
N 12 1948-1955
George Nakashima
W54", D32", H28.5". Birch wood,
natural, standard walnut, or ebony finish.
Photo Courtesy of the Knoll Museum.

Left:
Extension Table
112 1948-1949
Florence Knoll
W36", 54", H28". Extends to 72" with two leaves.
Birch top with walnut legs, natural finish.
Also shown: 130 Chairs.

Below:
"T" Angle Conference or Dining Table
300 1950
Florence Knoll
Dimensions unknown. Steel "T" angle base available
in a variety of finishes. Wood or plastic top, available
in a variety of finishes.

Above:
"T" Angle Coffee Table with Slate Top
115 1950-1951
Florence Knoll
W45", D22.5", H17". Steel "T" angle frame with slate top. Also available with teak wood top.

Left:
"T" Angle Dining Table
309 1952-1970
Florence Knoll
W34.5", D34", H28". Black, white, or woodgrain plastic top. Steel "T" angle base in a variety of finishes.
Also shown: 148 Stacking Chair introduced in 1961.

Above:
"T" Angle Coffee Table
306 1952-1968
Florence Knoll
W45", D23", H16". Black, white, or woodgrain plastic top. Steel "T" angle base in a variety of finishes.

"T" Angle End Table
304 1952-1970
Florence Knoll
W24", D24", H16". Black, white, or woodgrain plastic top. Steel "T" angle base in a variety of finishes.

"T" Angle Corner Table
305 1952-1970
Florence Knoll
W30", D30", H19". Black, white, or woodgrain plastic top. Steel "T" angle base in a variety of finishes.

Left:
"T" Angle Extension Table
310 F2 1954-1965
Florence Knoll
W34.5" extends to 48", D34", H28". Steel "T" angle base in a variety of finishes. Plastic top available in a variety of finishes.
Also shown: 72UPC Chairs.

Above:
"T" Angle End Table
308 1952-1970
Florence Knoll
W30", D30", H16". Black, white, or woodgrain plastic top. Steel "T" angle base in a variety of finishes.

"T" Angle Coffee Table
307 1/2 1952-1970
Florence Knoll
W48", D24", H16". Half black, half white plastic top. Steel "T" angle base in a variety of finishes.

"T" Angle Coffee Table
307 1952-1970
Florence Knoll
W45", D23", H16". Black, white, or woodgrain plastic top. Steel "T" angle base in a variety of finishes.

"T" Angle Outdoor Slat Dining Table
309 S 1958-1964
Florence Knoll
W34.5", D34", H28". Steel "T" angle base, available in various outdoor finishes. Redwood slat top.

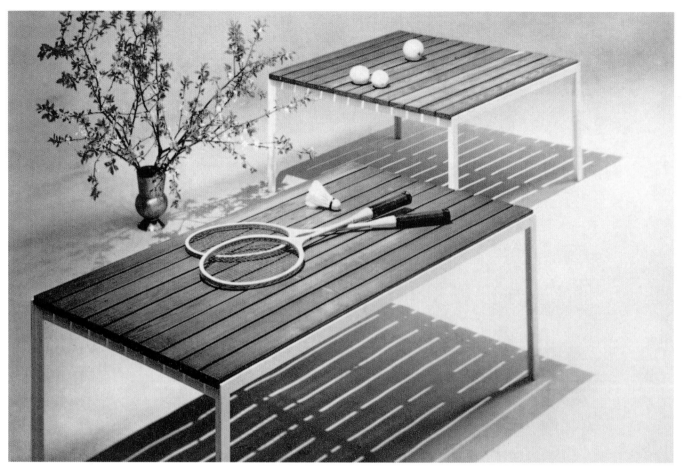

"T" Angle Outdoor Slat Coffee Table
308 S 1958-1964
Florence Knoll
W30", D30", H16". Steel "T" angle base, available in various
outdoor finishes. Redwood slat top.

"T" Angle Outdoor Slat Coffee Table
307 S 1958-1964
Florence Knoll
W45", D23", H16". Steel "T" angle base, available in various outdoor
finishes. Redwood slat top. 304, 305, 308 are also available with
redwood slat tops for outdoor use.

Slat Bench
400 R 1951-1971, 1987-1998
Harry Bertoia
W66", 72",82", D18.25",H15.5". Redwood top, other woods
and finishes available. Steel rod base, white fused plastic finish.
Other finishes available. Also available in solid ash with clear
lacquer or walnut finish and solid maple with ebony finish.

Parallel Bar Coffee Table
405 1955-1968
Florence Knoll
W42", D24", H16.5". Base, cross leg
steel bar , brushed chrome and black
finish. Polished 7/16" plate glass top.

"Parallel Bars" Round Coffee Table
404 1955-1968
Florence Knoll
Diam. 42", H15". Parallel bar steel base, brushed chrome and
black finish. Teak or walnut top, available in a variety of finishes.
Photo Courtesy of the Knoll Museum.

Barcelona Table
252 1954-1998
Ludwig Mies van der Rohe
W40", D40", H17". Stainless steel base.
Polished 3/4" plate glass top.

Coffee Table
355 1955-1970
Lewis Butler
W30", D30", H19". Walnut base and top
available in lacquer or oil finish.

Plank Top Table
360 1955-1956
Lewis Butler
W66", D20", H16". Walnut plank table top with maple legs.

Coffee Table
358 1955-1970
Lewis Butler
W38", D34", H16". Solid walnut base, available in a
variety of finishes. Plastic top with two white and two
black sections. *Photo Courtesy of the Knoll Museum.*

Children's Cyclone Table
87 1955-1975
Isamu Noguchi
Diam. 24", H20". Maple base, clear lacquer finish. Steel wire
column, black finish. Available with black or white plastic
laminate top. *Photo Courtesy of the Knoll Museum.*

"Cyclone" Dining Table
311 1955-1975
Isamu Noguchi
Diam. 36", H28.5". White plastic laminate top. Cast iron base
with black porcelain finish. Steel wire column, chrome plated
finish. Also available as 312 With 48" diameter top.
Photo Courtesy of the Knoll Museum.

Low Conference or Dining Table
352 W 1955-1968
Lewis Butler
Diam. 54", H25.5". Base and top walnut, with maple stretcher. Oil finish. Also available as 353 W Conference or Dining Table same as above but 28" high.

Conference Table
580 1952-1956
Florence Knoll
W40", L8', H28.5". Boat-shaped wood top in choice of maple, walnut, teak, cherry, or other by special order. Metal base with black oxide or black lacquer finish. Available in size from 8' to 26' long. Also available as 580 T1 with solid maple or walnut base, natural finish.
Also shown: 71 Arm Chairs.

Boat Shaped Conference Table
1581 1958-1976, 1987-1998
Florence Knoll
W40", L9'9", H28.5". Boat-shaped
wood top with beveled edge, in
walnut or other by special order.
Metal base with chrome finish. Base
also available with black lacquer
finish. Available in size from 8' to
26' long.
Also shown: 71UPC Arm Chairs.

Boat Shaped Conference Table
3581 1958-1976
Florence Knoll
W40", L9'9", H28.5". Boat-
shaped wood top with beveled
edge, in walnut or other by special
order. Walnut base available in a
variety of finishes. Available in size
from 8' to 26' long.
Also shown: 71 Arm Chairs.

"T" Angle Bench
332 1956-1971
Florence Knoll
W80.5", D20", H15.5. Walnut top, available in a variety of finishes. Steel "T" angle base, black finish. White and other finishes available. Also available in 40", and 60" lengths.

Pedestal Conference Table
175 R 1957-1998
Eero Saarinen
W96", D54", H28.5". Cast metal base, walnut veneer top with oil finish. Also shown: 150 US Arm Chair.

Single Pedestal Side Table
160 MC 1957-1998
Eero Saarinen
(Upper left) Diam.16", H20.5". Cast metal base, Italian
Cremo Marble top.

Round Small Pedestal Coffee Table
162 MW 1957-1998
Eero Saarinen
(Right) Diam. 36", H15". Cast metal base, Wallen Grey
Marble top.

Oval Pedestal Coffee Table
167 W 1957-1998
Eero Saarinen
(Left) W54", D36", H15.25". Cast metal base with
charcoal finish. Walnut veneer top.

Single Pedestal Side Table
163 F 1957-1998
Eero Saarinen
(Bottom center) Diam. 20", H20.5". Cast metal base,
white plastic laminate top.

Round Medium Pedestal Dining Table
173 M 1957-1998
Eero Saarinen
(Top center) Diam. 42", H28". Cast metal base. White
Italian Marble top, with grey vein.

Left:
Oval Single Pedestal Dining Table
174 M 1957-1996
Eero Saarinen
W78", D48", H28.5". Cast metal base. White Italian
marble top, with grey vein. Also shown: 151S Side Chair.

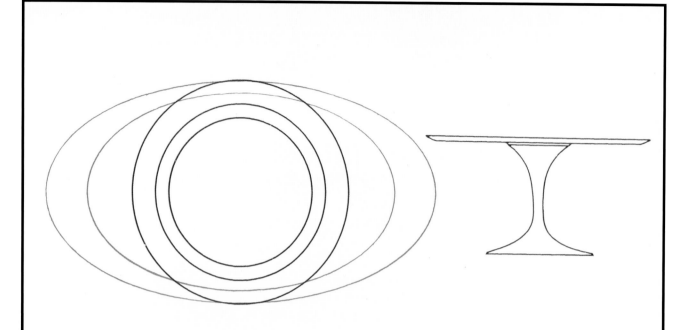

DINING OR CONFERENCE TABLES

item no.	description	specifications	dimensions w d h
172W 172F 172M 172MW 172MC	**SMALL DINING TABLE—ROUND**	Top: W—Walnut veneer, oil finish F—White plastic laminate M—White Italian Marble, grey vein, honed finish	36" diameter 28"
173W 173F 173M 173MW 173MC	**MEDIUM DINING TABLE—ROUND**	MW—Wallen Grey Marble, high polish MC—Italian Cremo Marble, high polish Base: Pedestal base, cast metal, in white, grey or	42" diameter 28"
164W 164F 164M 164MW 164MC	**LARGE DINING TABLE—ROUND**	charcoal finish. Specify color when ordering.	54" diameter 28"
174W 174F 174M 174MW 174MC	**MEDIUM DINING TABLE—OVAL**		78" x 48" x 28½"
175W 175F	**LARGE DINING TABLE—OVAL**		96" x 54" x 28½"

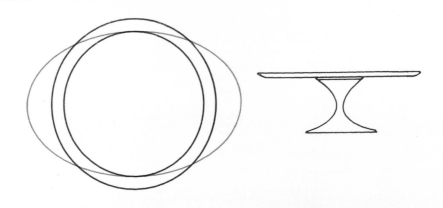

COFFEE TABLES

item no.	description	specifications	dimensions w d h

162W
162F
162M
162MW
162MC
	SMALL COFFEE TABLE—ROUND	Top: W—Walnut veneer, oil finish
		    F—White plastic laminate
		    M—White Italian Marble, grey vein, honed finish
			36″ diameter 15″

166W 166F 166M 166MW 166MC	**LARGE COFFEE TABLE—ROUND**	MW—Wallen Grey Marble, high polish MC—Italian Cremo Marble, high polish	42″ diameter 15″
167W 167F 167M 167MW 167MC	**COFFEE TABLE—OVAL**	Base: Pedestal base, cast metal, in white, grey or charcoal finish. Specify color when ordering.	36″ x 54″ x 15″

SIDE AND OCCASIONAL TABLES

160W 160F 160M 160MW 160MC	**SMALL SIDE TABLE—ROUND**		16″ diameter 20″
163W 163F 163M 163MW 163MC	**SIDE TABLE—ROUND**		20″ diameter 20½″
161W 161F 161M 161MW 161MC	**SMALL SIDE TABLE—OVAL**		15″ x 22½″ x 20″

Rectangular Conference Table
3570 WR 1958-1971
Designer unknown
W76", D36", H28.5". Walnut
base available in a variety of
finishes. Walnut plastic top,
available in a variety of finishes.

Rectangular Conference Table
1570 WR 1958-1971
Designer unknown
W76", D36", H28.5". Steel
base, brushed chrome finish.
Other finishes available.
Walnut plastic top, available in
a variety of finishes.

Coffee Table
2518 RW 1958-1975
Florence Knoll
(Center) W36", D36", H17". Square
tubular base, brushed chrome finish. Other
finishes available. Rosewood top available
in a variety of finishes and materials,
including teak, cremo marble, and white
marble with grey vein.

End Table
2510 WV 1958-1976
Florence Knoll
(Top) W24", D24", H17". Square tubular
base, brushed chrome finish with black
steel angle spacers. Other finishes available.
Walnut top available in a variety of finishes
and materials, including teak, rosewood,
and white marble with grey vein.

End Table
2514 MC 1958-1976
Florence Knoll
(Bottom) W27", D27", H17". Square
tubular base, brushed chrome finish. Other
finishes available. Cremo marble top
available in a variety of finishes and
materials, including teak, rosewood, and
white marble with grey vein.

Coffee Table
2511 MC 1958-1976
Florence Knoll
W45", D23", H17". Tubular base, brushed chrome finish. Other
finishes available. Cremo marble top. Top available in a variety of
finishes and materials, including teak, rosewood, and white marble
with grey vein.

Side Table
2562 T 1958-1976
Florence Knoll
Diam 25", H14". Square tubular steel base with brushed
chrome finish. Teak top, available in a variety of finishes and
materials, including walnut, cremo marble, rosewood, and white
marble with grey vein.

Petal Dining Table
322 R 1960-1975
Richard Schultz
Diam. 42", H28". Metal base, white fused plastic finish. Eight section redwood petal top, available in a variety of finishes. Suitable for indoor and outdoor use. Also available as 322 painted top.

Petal Side Table
The Petal Table series won the design award from *Industrial Design* Magazine in 1961.
320 R 1960-1975
Richard Schultz
(Bottom) Diam. 16", H19". Metal base, white fused plastic finish. Eight section redwood petal top, available in a variety of finishes. Suitable for indoor and outdoor use. Also available as 320 P with painted top.

Petal Coffee Table
321 P 1960-1975
Richard Schultz
(Top) Diam. 42", H16". Metal base, white fused plastic finish. Wooden eight section white petal top, available in a variety of finishes. Also available with redwood top.
Also shown: 421 Small Diamond Chair.

Cabinets

Cabinet
NK1 1947-1950
Elias Svedberg
W37.5", D17.5", H31.5". Swing doors with lock, two sliding shelves.
Cabinet elm with natural finish. Base and legs birch with natural finish.
Manufactured in Sweden by Nordiska Kompaniet.

Chest
NK3 1947-1950
Elias Svedberg
W37.5", D17.5", H31.5". Three drawers with one lock. Cabinet elm
with natural finish. Base and legs birch with natural finish. Manufactured
in Sweden by Nordiska Kompaniet.

Wall Desk
NK10 1947-1950
Elias Svedberg
Shown with swinging door open.
Also Shown: 60S Chair.

Above:
Wall Desk
NK10 1947-1950
Elias Svedberg
(Center) W33.5", D9.75", H26". Hinged door with lock, partitions inside. Elm natural finish. Manufactured in Sweden by Nordiska Kompaniet.

Wall Bookcase
NK12 1947-1950
Elias Svedberg
(Left) W33.5", D9.75", H26". Elm with natural finish. Manufactured in Sweden by Nordiska Kompaniet.

Wall Dressing Table
NK11 1947-1950
Elias Svedberg
(Right) W33.5", D9.75", H26". Hinged door with lock, partitions and mirror inside. Elm with natural finish. Manufactured in Sweden by Nordiska Kompaniet. Also shown 652W Chair and NK7 Table.

Left:
Wall Dressing Table
NK11 1947-1950
Elias Svedberg
Shown with swinging door open.
Also Shown: 667W Stool.

Cabinet
120 1947-1949
Florence Knoll
W72", D15", H32.25". Birch cabinet with natural finish. Inside white enamel.
Base walnut finish. Three adjustable wood shelves, two adjustable glass shelves.
Saddle leather pulls. Also shown: 654 Chair.

Cabinet
122 1947-1949
Florence Knoll
W72", D15", H32.25". Birch or maple cabinet with natural finish. Sliding doors
covered in "Pandanus". Inside white enamel with three adjustable wood shelves,
two adjustable glass shelves. Base finish walnut. Saddle leather pulls.

Hanging Cabinet
121 1947-1973
Florence Knoll
W72", D15.25", H17.75". Birch or maple case available in a variety of
finishes. Drop front doors. Inside white enamel. Three adjustable wood
shelves, two adjustable glass shelves. Saddle leather pulls.
Also shown: 654U Chair, 198 Hardoy Chair, N11 Table, and 700 Daybed.

Hanging Cabinet
123 1947-1973
Florence Knoll
W72", D15.25", H17.75". Birch or maple case available in a variety of
finishes. White lacquered interior with three adjustable wood shelves
and two adjustable glass shelves.

Hanging Cabinet
123 W-1 1947-1973
Florence Knoll
(Left) W72", D15.25", H17.75". Walnut or birch case available in a variety of finishes. White lacquered sliding doors, available in a variety of finishes. White lacquered interior with three adjustable wood shelves and two adjustable glass shelves.

Hanging Cabinet
121 W-1 1947-1973
Florence Knoll
(Right) W72", D15.25", H17.75". Walnut or birch case available in a variety of finishes. White lacquered drop doors, available in a variety of finishes. White lacquered interior with three adjustable wood shelves and two adjustable glass shelves. Saddle leather pulls.

Sideboard
116 1948-1964
Florence Knoll
W72", D18", H31". Case in birch, maple, walnut, or ebonized. Inside white lacquer finish. Felt lined silver drawer seven adjustable shelves. Caned sliding doors with saddle leather pulls. Tubular steel legs with black finish. Legs also available in polished or brushed chrome.

Cabinet
540 1952-1978
Florence Knoll
(Right) W36", D17.75", H27.5". Square tubular steel legs, black finish.
Other finishes available. Shown in walnut, available in a variety of woods
and finishes. Four adjustable wood shelves. Available in a hanging
version 20" high. Optional file and tray drawers and sliding dictating
machine shelf available.

Cabinet
541 1952-1983
Florence Knoll
(Left) W72", D17.75", H27.5". Square tubular steel legs, black finish.
Other finishes available. Shown in walnut, available in a variety of
woods and finishes. Eight adjustable wood shelves. Also available as
542 WV - 48" wide. Both are also available in a hanging version 20" high.

Bedroom Furniture

Chest
125 1948-1956
Florence Knoll
(Not Shown) W 36", D18", H28". Three drawer birch chest with natural, standard walnut, or ebony finish. Birch legs available with natural, standard walnut, or ebony finish. Also available in maple.

Chest
126 1948-1956
Florence Knoll
W36", D18", H34.75". Four drawer birch chest with natural, standard walnut, or ebony finish. Birch legs available with natural, standard walnut, or ebony finish. Also available in maple.

Chest
127 1948-1956
Florence Knoll
(Not Shown) W 18", D18", H28". Three drawer birch chest with natural, standard walnut, or ebony finish. Birch legs available with natural, standard walnut, or ebony finish. Also available in maple.

Chest
137 1953-1956
Florence Knoll
(Left) W 18", D18", H28". Chest case available in birch natural, standard walnut, or ebony finish. All drawer fronts black or white finish. Also available in maple. Metal legs with black finish.

Chest
135 1953-1956
Florence Knoll
(Center) W 36", D18", H28". Chest case available in birch natural, standard walnut, or ebony finish. All drawer fronts black or white finish. Also available in maple. Metal legs with black finish. Also available as 155, two three drawer chests on a single base.

Chest
136 1953-1956
Florence Knoll
(Right) W36", D18", H34.75". Chest case available in birch natural, standard walnut, or ebony finish. All drawer fronts black or white finish. Also available in maple. Metal legs with black finish.

Above:
Luggage Rack and Chests
128 1950-1956
Florence Knoll
W108", D18", H33.25". Birch chests rest on wooden bench with tubular metal legs and webbed top section. Available in a variety of finishes. Contract only.
Also shown: 130 Chair.

Left:
Chest with Desk Compartment
130 1950-1956
Florence Knoll
(Right) W33", D18", H33.25". Contract only.

Chest with Dressing Table Compartment
129 1950-1956
Florence Knoll
(Left) W33", D18", H33.25". Contract only.

Three Drawer Chest
225 -3 1956-1959?
Knoll Planning Unit
W37", D19.5", H29.25". Natural teak
chest, finished on all sides. Drawers have
metal slides.

Three Drawer Chest
225 -2 1956-1959?
Knoll Planning Unit
W37", D19.5", H29.25". Teak
and white plastic laminate,
finished on all sides. Drawers
have metal slides.

Vanity
229 -1 1956-1959?
Knoll Planning Unit
(Center) W28", D19.5". Teak case with white plastic top.
Also shown: 62 Ottoman.

Four Drawer Chest
226 -1 1956-1959?
Knoll Planning Unit
(Left and Right) W37", D19.5", H29.25". Natural teak chest, finished
on all sides. White plastic top. Drawers have metal slides.

Four Drawer Chest
226 -2 1956-1959?
Knoll Planning Unit
W37", D19.5", H29.25". Teak and white plastic laminate,
finished on all sides. Drawers have metal slides.

137

Left:
Bed Table
227 -1 1956-1959?
Richard Schultz
W19.5", D19.5", H18". Teak case and drawer, available in a variety of finishes. White plastic top available in a variety of finishes.

Below:
Three Drawer Chest
323 -2 1960-1973
Florence Knoll
W36", D19.5", H29.25". Walnut case and drawers with satin aluminum pulls, available in a variety of finishes. Walnut top. Available in a variety of finishes. Also available as 323-1 with white plastic top.

Four Drawer Chest
325 -1 1960-1973
Florence Knoll
W36", D19.5", H36.5". Walnut case and drawers with satin
aluminum pulls, available in a variety of finishes. White plastic top.
Available in a variety of finishes. Also available as 325-2 with
walnut plastic top.

Four Drawer Chest
324 -2 1960-1973
Florence Knoll
W36", D19.5", H29.25". Walnut case and drawers with satin
aluminum pulls, available in a variety of finishes. Walnut top.
Available in a variety of finishes.

Five Drawer Chest
326 -2 1960-1973
Florence Knoll
W36", D19.5", H36.5". Walnut case and drawers with satin
aluminum pulls, available in a variety of finishes. Walnut top.
Available in a variety of finishes. Also available as 326-1 with
white plastic top.

Suspended Vanity
329 -1 1960-1973
Florence Knoll
(Center) W28", D19.5", H4.5". Walnut front, available in a variety of
finishes. White plastic top, available in a variety of finishes. Separate tray
insert available. Also available as 329-2 with walnut top.
Also shown: 62 Ottoman.

Four Drawer Chest
324 -1 1960-1973
Florence Knoll
(Left and Right) W36", D19.5", H29.25". Walnut case and drawers with
satin aluminum pulls, available in a variety of finishes. White plastic top .
Available in a variety of finishes.

Bed Table
327 -1S 1956-1973
Florence Knoll
W19.5", D19.5", H18". Walnut
case, drawer, and shelf, available
in a variety of finishes. White
plastic top available in a variety
of finishes. Bed table also
available without shelf as 327-1.
Also available as 327-2S with
walnut top.

Headboard
740 WP 1956-1968
Florence Knoll
W40", H29.5". Walnut frame,
white plastic panel. Caned or
plastic panels available. Beds and
headboards available in other
widths.

Headboard Series
740 1956-1970
Florence Knoll
W40", H16". 740WF, Walnut frame ,
fabric covered panel. 740WC, Walnut
frame , caned panel. 740F, Fully upholstered. 740WP (not shown) Walnut
frame, white plastic panel. All headboards available in 55" and 81" widths
and equipped with mounting brackets.

Single Bed
704 1950
Florence Knoll and Knoll Planning
Unit W36", D75.5", H27". Metal
frame bed with padded headboard
and innerspring mattress with
foam rubber. Also available as 705
Double Bed. Also shown: 75
Stacking Stool.

Single Bed
721 H 1956-1964
Richard Schultz
W76", D38.25", H29.75". Foam
mattress on coil spring platform
with walnut legs. Attached tilting
headboard has walnut frame with
caned panel. Beds and headboards
available in other widths. Also
available as 722H Double Bed
W76", D53", H29.75". Headboard
in two sections on 722.

Daybed
700 1947-1961
Richard Stein, Product Design Associates
W76", D34", H27". Birch or maple base with clear lacquer, walnut, or ebony finish. Foam rubber mattress over plywood platform. Movable upholstered foam rubber back operated by foot pedal under seat. Also shown: N11 Coffee Table and Cartree.

Convertible Sofa Bed
701 1950-1954
Florence Knoll, Charles Niedringhaus
W83.5", D36", H31". Back pivots away from foam rubber
mattress for sleeping. Also available 702 same as 701 but
30" deep. Also shown: NK8 Table, 92 Scissor Chair.

Convertible Sofa Bed
703 BC 1958-1970
Richard Schultz
W76", D31.75", H28.5". Square tubular steel base , brushed chrome finish. Other finishes available. Seat pulls forward on counterbalanced rollers to horizontal position.
Also shown: 166F Pedestal Table.

Convertible Sofa Bed with Arms
704 BC 1958-1970
Richard Schultz
W82", D31.75", H28.5". Square tubular steel base , brushed chrome finish. Other finishes available. Seat pulls forward to horizontal position.

Desks

Desk
NK 2 1947-1950
Elias Svedberg
W50", D29", H28.75". Two
drawers one with lock, one with
pencil rack. Cabinet elm with
natural finish. Base and legs birch
with natural finish. Manufactured in
Sweden by Nordiska Kompaniet.
Also shown: 666W Chair.

Secretarial Desk
14 1947-1951
Designer unknown
W64", D28", H29". Birch plywood with
walnut legs. Natural finish. Also available
as 14W all walnut. Available with center
modesty panel.
Also shown: T60U Work Chair.

Above:
Executive Desk
13 W 1947-1951
Designer unknown
W78", D36", H29". Walnut with natural finish.
Also available as 13 birch plywood with walnut
legs. Also shown: 44S Swivel Chair.

Left:
Double Pedestal Desk
16 1947-1951
Florence Knoll
W64", D30", H29". Birch plywood with walnut
legs. Natural finish. Also available as 16W all
walnut. Available with center modesty panel.
Also shown: 48 Chair.

Single Pedestal Desk
15 1947-1960
Florence Knoll
W50", D28", H29". Birch plywood with walnut legs. Natural finish.
Also available as 15W all walnut. *Photo Courtesy of the Knoll Museum.*

Single Pedestal Desk
17 1947-1956
Designer unknown
W48", D24", H29". Birch with birch legs. Natural finish.
Also available in maple. Also shown: 146 Chair.

Desk
80 1949-1954, 1987, 1996-1998
Franco Albini
W48", D26", H28". Metal frame desk with birch drawer unit and glass
top. Reintroduced in 1987 with chrome plated frame and legs.
Also shown: 47 Desk Chair

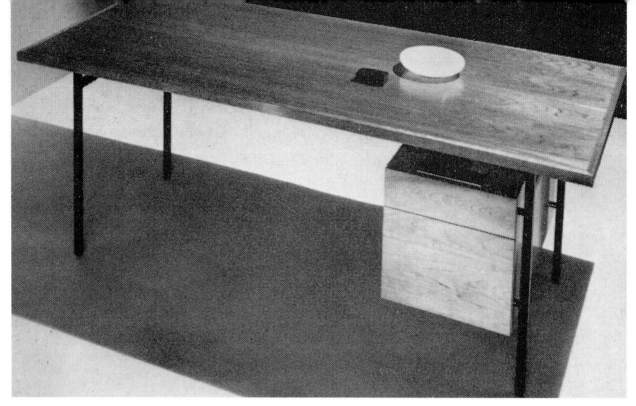

Large Executive Desk
503 D-BM 1952-1955
Florence Knoll
(Not Shown) W76", D36", H29". Birch Realwood top with
one small drawer with pencil tray. Metal base with black
finish. Also available with walnut top or top and drawer.

Large Executive Desk
503 B-BM 1952-1955
Florence Knoll
W76", D36", H29". Birch Realwood top with one pedestal.
Metal base with black finish. Also available with walnut top
or top and pedestal.

Large Executive Desk
503 A-BM 1952-1955
Florence Knoll
W76", D36", H29". Birch Realwood top with two pedestals.
Metal base with black finish. Also available with walnut top or
top and pedestals.

Knoll Furniture

Knoll Fabrics

Knoll Planning Unit

KNOLL ASSOCIATES, INC., 575 MADISON AVENUE, NEW YORK 22, N.Y.

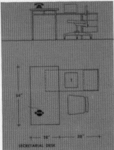

SECRETARIAL DESKS from the Knoll Office Planned Furniture Group. The new L-shape design provides maximum work area per square foot of space and brings wider flexibility to the planning of contemporary offices. Structural base of black metal supports a burn and stain-proof, high pressure laminate top of linen or birch, with stepped-down typewriter extension left or right. Grouped in multiples of two or more, these desks form working units of great efficiency in compact space. Knoll Office Planned Furniture is available in integrated groups of desks, tables, cabinets and chairs for executives and secretaries. Information on request.

T-TYPEWRITER
D-DICTAPHONE

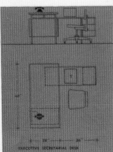

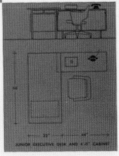

L-Shaped Secretarial Desk
500 PM 1952-1955
Florence Knoll
(Top) Main Top, W54", D28", H29". Typewriter platform, W38", D20", H24.5". Grey linen Panelyte top, single pedestal with three drawers, birch natural finish. Metal base black finish. Also available with birch Realwood top.

L-Shaped Executive Secretarial Desk
501 PM 1952-1955
Florence Knoll
(Left) Main Top, W60", D28", H29". Typewriter platform, W36", D17", H24.5". Grey linen Panelyte top, double pedestal , birch natural finish. Two drawers in large pedestal and three drawers in typewriter platform. Metal base black finish. Also available with birch Realwood top.

Small Executive Desk
502 B-BWM 1952-1955
Florence Knoll
(Right) W66", D32", H29". Walnut Realwood top with walnut pedestal. Metal base with black finish. Also available with birch top and pedestal. Also shown: 542W Cabinet.

Double Pedestal Desk
1503 E 1955-1983
Florence Knoll
W76", D36", H29". Square tubular steel base, brushed chrome finish. Black finish available. Case and drawers ebonized finish, also available in maple or walnut . Top plastic walnut, available in a variety of finishes. Available as right or left single pedestal desk. Also available with wood base.

Small Executive Desk
1517 1955-1983
Florence Knoll
W76", D36", H29". Square tubular steel base, black finish. Also available in brushed chrome finish. Maple case and drawers natural finish, also available in maple or ebonized. Maple plastic top, other finishes available. Also available with wood base.
Also shown: 542 Cabinet and 72 Swivel Chair.

Small Executive Desk
1513 WR 1955-1983
Florence Knoll
W66", D32", H29". Square tubular steel base, black finish.
Brushed chrome finish available. Walnut case and drawers, also
available in maple or ebonized. Walnut plastic top, available in
a variety of finishes. Also available with wood base.

Double Pedestal Secretarial Desk
1523 W 1955-1960?
Florence Knoll
W60", D30", H29". Square tubular steel base, black finish. Also
available in brushed chrome finish. Walnut case and drawers, also
available in maple or ebonized. Walnut plastic top available in a variety
of finishes. Also available with wood base.

Double Pedestal L-Shaped Secretarial Desk
1543 W 1955-1983
Florence Knoll
Main Desk- W66", D32", H29". Typewriter Platform- W43.5",
D19.25", H26.25". Square tubular steel base black finish. Brushed
chrome finish also available. Walnut case and drawers also available in
maple or ebonized. Walnut plastic tops available in a variety.
Also shown: 76 Secretarial Swivel Chair.

153

Accessories

8

9

Above:
Desk Lamp
8 1950-1960
Clay Michie
Diam. 12", H18". Brushed brass plated base, metal shade with swivel.

Below:
Table Lamp
9 1947-1967
Isamu Noguchi
Diam. 7.25", H16". Translucent plastic shade on cherrywood supports.

Right:
Single Letter Tray
1 1948-1978
Florence Knoll
W11.5", D14", H2 1/4". Molded birch plywood also
available in walnut or ebony finish.

1

Below:
Double Letter Tray
2 1948-1978
Florence Knoll
W11.5", D14", H7". Two molded birch plywood
trays connected with metal pivot.
Also available in walnut or ebony.

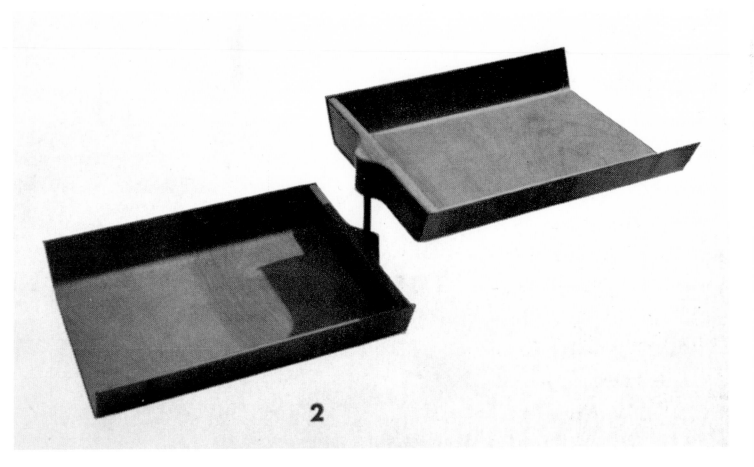

2

Bibliography

Books

Beer, Eileen Harrison. *Scandinavian Design Objects of a Life Style*. New York, 1975.

Byars, Mel. *The Design Encyclopedia*. New York: John Wiley & Sons, Inc.,1994.

Candee, Marjorie Dent, ed. *Current Biography (Yearbook 1955)*. New York: The H.H. Wilson Company., 1955.

Eidelberg, Martin, ed. *Design 1935-1965 :What Modern Was*. New York: Harry N. Abrams, Inc., 1981.

Fiell, Charlotte and Peter Fiell. *Modern Chairs*, Köln: Taschen,1993.

Fiell, Charlotte and Peter Fiell. *Modern Furniture Classics Since 1945*. Washington: The American Institute of Architects Press, 1991.

Grant, Tina, ed. *International Directory of Company Histories (Vol. 14)*. U.S.A. and United Kingdom: St. James Press., 1996.

Habegger, Jerryll and Joseph H. Osman. *Sourcebook of Modern Furniture*. New York: W.W. Norton Company, Inc., 1997.

Hiesinger, Kathryn B., and George H. Marcus, eds. *Design since 1945*. Philadephia, 1983.

Larrabee, Eric and Massimo Vignelli. *Knoll Design*. New York: Harry N. Abrams, Inc., 1981.

Meeus, Cathy. *The Illustrated Dictionary of Twentieth Century Designers*. New York: Mallard Press, 1991.

Morgan, Lee Ann. *Contemporary Designers*. New York: MacMillan Publishers Ltd., 1984.

Neuhart, John, Marilyn Neuhart, and Ray Eames. *Eames Design*. New York: Harry N. Abrams, Inc., 1989.

Pile, John. *Dictionary of 20th-Century Design*. Roundtable Press, Inc.,1990.

Spaeth, David. *Mies van der Rohe*. New York: Rizzoli International Publications, Inc. 1985.

Company Sources

Bode, Peter M., Nick Jordan and Mel Silver, *Knoll 50 Years of Design*. West Germany: AWS/WWS YY-B50Y, 1987.

Chairs by Harry Bertoia, Knoll Associates Inc., 1966

H.G. Knoll Associates, furniture catalog, undated

H.G. Knoll Associates, furniture catalog with price list, November 1, 1946

Knoll Archive Catalog, July 27, 1998

Knoll Associates, Inc., brochure yellow, undated

Knoll Associates, Inc., catalog, 1947-1948

Knoll Associates, Inc., catalog, 1948-1949

Knoll Associates, Inc., catalog, 1962

Knoll Associates, Inc., catalog, undated

Knoll Associates, Inc., furniture price list, September 1,1961

Knoll Associates, Inc., furniture price list, July 15, 1964

Knoll Associates, Inc., furniture price list, October 15, 1968

Knoll Associates, Inc., mailer red, undated

Knoll Associates, Inc., mailer yellow, undated

Knoll Associates, Inc., price list addenda, May 18, 1948

Knoll Associates, Inc., price list, February 10, 1948

Knoll Associates, Inc., price list, April 15, 1953

Knoll Associates, Inc., price list, December 20,1951

Knoll Associates, Inc., Furniture, Textiles, Planning, with price list, January 1,1951

Knoll, 1949

Knoll Associates, Inc., price list, January 1, 1954

Knoll Associates, Inc., price list, January 9, 1956

Knoll Associates, Inc., Saarinen Pedestal Collection, 1966

Knoll Associates, Inc., supplementary price list, August 1, 1958

Knoll Associates, Inc., supplementary price list, August 1, 1962

Knoll Associates, Inc., supplementary price list, February 15, 1967

Knoll, Authorized Federal Supply Schedule Catalog/Price List, January18,1972-December 31, 1972

Knoll Furniture Guide, A Condensed Guide to the Knoll International Furniture Collection, undated

Knoll Furniture Catalog, ring binder, undated

Knoll Furniture price list, March 1982

Knoll Furniture price list, June 1983

Knoll Index of Design, 1950

Knoll International Furniture and Textiles, 1971

Knoll International Furniture Catalog and Price List 3/87

Knoll International furniture price list 1977/78 Contract Residential, November 15, 1977

Knoll International furniture price list 1977-1978 Residential, November 15, 1977

Knoll International furniture price list 5/79 Contract Residential, May 1, 1979

Knoll International furniture price list 10/79, October 1, 1979

Knoll International furniture price list 4/80, April 1, 1980

Knoll International furniture price list 2/81, February 1, 1981

Knoll International, Inc., furniture price list, December 1, 1969

Knoll International, Inc., furniture price list, May 15, 1971

Knoll International, Inc., furniture price list, April 1, 1973

Knoll International, Inc., furniture price list, June 1, 1974

Knoll International, Inc., interim price list, January 1, 1975

Knoll International, Inc., furniture price list, September 15, 1976

Knoll International residential price list 10/79, October 1, 1979

Knoll International, The Collections, Furniture Catalog and Price List 2/91

Knoll Office Planned Furniture, 1956

Knoll price list update, April 1985

Knoll Residential/Fine Furniture price list, June 1984

KnollStudio, Price List 1988

KnollStudio, Price List 1990

KnollStudio, Price List 1991

KnollStudio, Price List 1992-1994
KnollStudio, Price List March 1996
KnollStudio, Price List 1998
KnollStudio, The Bertoia Collection, 1988
New Outdoor Furniture, Petal Tables by Richard Schultz, Knoll Associates Inc.
Nordiska Kompaniet Furniture catalog, with price list, November 1,1949
The Morrison/Hannah Collection, 1973

Exhibition Catalogs

Knoll au Louvre, Pavillon de Marsan, January-March 1972.
Ralph Rapson: Sixty Years of Modern Design, The Minneapolis Institute of Arts, March 27- July 25, 1999. (by Jane King Hession, Rip Rapson, and Bruce Wright, published by Afton Historical Society Presses: Afton, Minnesota, 1999)

Internet

"Warburg, Pincus Signs Agreement to Buy Knoll," desigNEWS: January, 1996. @ http://www.isdesignet.com.
"Knoll," @ www.knoll.com.

Magazines

Anderson, John. "The continuities of Jens Risom," *Interiors*, CXIX (October 1959), 150-155,220-222.
Bassett, Florence Knoll, "The Interiors at CBS," *Office Design* (May 1966).
"Earmarked for manufacture in the United States," *Interiors*, (July 1948), 70.
"George Nakashima His Furniture His House His Way of Life" *House and Home*, (March 1952), 80-89.
Gueft, Olga. "Outpost in Dallas Knoll opens a Lone Star branch," *Interiors*, CIX (June 1950), 90-97.

Gueft, Olga. "Knoll Associates move into the big time," *Interiors*, CX (May 1951), 74-83,152,154 & 156.
Gueft, Olga. "Florence Knoll and the avant garde," *Interiors*, CXVI (July 1957), 59-66.
Gueft, Olga. "Knoll without Knolls?" *Interiors*, (August 1966), 150-157.
Interiors, (August 1942),84.
Interiors, (March 1947), 78.
Interiors, (August 1947)
Jespersen, Mark. "An Interview with Jens Risom," *The Echoes Report*, 4 ({Fall 1995), 32,33,54.
"Knoll Associates, Drum Beaters for Modern," *Life*, 34 (2 March 1953), 72-76.
"Knoll Exhibits Work of A.I.A. Craftsmanship Medal Winnner," *Architectural Record*, 112 (July 1952).
"Modern doesn't pay, or does it," *Interiors*, (March 1946), 66-75.
"Museum Watch," *Echoes*, 7 (Winter 1998), 34.
Olivarez, Jennifer Komar. "Ralph Rapson and Hans Knoll," *Echoes*, 7 (Summer 1998), 48-51 & 74-75.
Rudofsky, Bernard. "Fifty pages of postwar furniture and interiors from Italy," *Interiors*, CVII (July 1948),70.

Newspapers

Freeman, William M. "She Designs Offices Outside In." *The New York Times*, 15 October 1957, p.45.
Warren, Virginia Lee. "Woman Who Led an Office Revolution Rules an Empire." *The New York Times*, 1 September 1964, p.40.

Video

National Public Television's American Masters, "Noguchi."

Identification, Price Guide & Index

Model Number	Description	Production Date	Value	Page
97-2	Settee	1954-1970	600-800	80
97-1	Settee	1953-1970	600-1000	78
100	Coffee Table	1947-1950	100-200	101
102	Dinette Table	1947-1949	150-300	104
103	Small Tripod Table	1947-1961	800-1300	102
106	Stacking Table	1948-1964	300-500	106
108	Sofa Table	1948	1500-2000	104
110	Coffee Table	1948-1954	500-1000	106
112	Extension Table	1948-1949	700-900	108
114	Large Tripod Table	1947-1954	900-1500	103
115	'T" Angle Coffee Table with Slate Top	1950-1951	900-1500	109
116	Sideboard	1948-1964	500-900	132
120	Cabinet	1947-1949	1500-2000	130
121W-1	Hanging Cabinet	1947-1973	500-800	132
121	Hanging Cabinet	1947-1973	1200-1500	131
122	Cabinet	1947-1949	1200-1500	130
123 W-1	Hanging Cabinet	1947-1973	400-600	132
123	Hanging Cabinet	1947-1973	600-900	131
125	Chest	1948-1956	600-800	134
126	Chest	1948-1956	600-800	134
127	Chest	1948-1956	200-300	134
128	Luggage Rack and Chests	1950-1956	1800-2500	135
129**	Chest with Dressing Table Compartment	1950-1956	INC	135
130**	Chest with Desk Compartment	1950-1956	INC	135
130	Stacking Chair	1947-1966	200-300	
132	Metal Chair	1950-1952		56
135	Chest	1953-1956	600-800	134
136	Chest	1953-1956	600-800	134
137	Chest	1953-1956	200-300	134
141	Stacking Chair	1947-1962	75-150	48
145	Side Chair	1954-1960	150-250	61
146	Side Chair	1950-1953	100-200	54
147	Arm Chair	1950-1953	100-200	54
150	Pedestal Arm Chair	1956-1998	150-350	63
150 DS	Swivel Arm Chair	1956-1998	150-350	65
150 U	Pedestal Arm Chair	1956-1998	150-350	64
151	Pedestal Side Chair	1956-1996	100-250	63
151 UDS	Swivel Side Chair	1956-1998	100-250	64
151 DS	Swivel Side Chair	1956-1998	100-250	64
151 U	Pedestal Side Chair	1956-1998	100-250	64
152 S	Pedestal Stool	1957-1984	200-350	65
160 MC	Single Pedestal Side Table	1957-1998	300-500	121
162 MW	Round Small Pedestal Coffee Table	1957-1998	300-500	121
163 F	Single Pedestal Side Table	1957-1998	200-400	121
167 W	Oval Pedestal Coffee Table	1957-1998	200-400	121
173 M	Round Medium Pedestal Dining Table	1957-1998	900-1200	121
174 M	Oval Single Pedestal Dining Table	1957-1996	2000-3000	120
175 R	Pedestal Conference Table	1957-1998	1000-1500	119
198 L	Hardoy Chair	1947-1950	150-300	48
201	Armless Chair	1947-1951	400-600	68
225-3	Three Drawer Chest	1956-1959?	600-800	136
225-2	Three Drawer Chest	1956-1959?	600-800	136
226-1	Four Drawer Chest	1956-1959?	600-800	137
226-2	Four Drawer Chest	1956-1959?	600-800	137
227-1	Bed Table	1956-1959?	150-300	138
229-1	Vanity	1956-1959?	200-300	137
250	Barcelona Chair	1948-1998	800-1200	80
251	Barcelona Stool	1954-1998	500-1000	81
252	Barcelona Table	1954-1998	500-700	114
253	Barcelona Stool	1954-1978	500-1000	81
300	'T" Angle Conference or Dining Table	1950	500-900	108

Model Number	Description	Production Date	Value	Page
301	Extension Dining Table	1950-1956	200-400	105
302	"Popsicle" Dining Table	1947-1956		105
304	'T" Angle End Table	1952-1970		110
305	'T" Angle Corner Table	1952-1970	125-250	110
306	'T" Angle Coffee Table	1952-1968	250-350	110
307 1/2	'T" Angle Coffee Table	1952-1970	200-300	111
307	'T" Angle Coffee Table	1952-1970	200-300	111
307 S	'T" Angle Outdoor Slat Coffee Table	1958-1964	300-500	112
308 S	'T" Angle Outdoor Slat Coffee Table	1958-1964	300-500	112
308	'T" Angle End Table	1952-1970	125-250	111
309	'T" Angle Dining Table	1952-1970	300-500	109
309 S	'T" Angle Outdoor Slat Dining Table	1958-1964	300-500	111
310 F2	'T" Angle Extension Table	1954-1965	700-1100	110
311	"Cyclone" Dining Table	1955-1975	1000-1500	116
320 R	Petal Side Table	1960-1975	400-600	127
321 P	Petal Coffee Table	1960-1975	600-1200	127
322 R	Petal Dining Table	1960-1975	600-1200	126
323-2	Three Drawer Chest	1960-1973	600-800	138
324-1	Four Drawer Chest	1960-1973	600-800	140
324-2	Four Drawer Chest	1960-1973	600-800	139
325-1	Four Drawer Chest	1960-1973	600-800	139
326-2	Five Drawer Chest	1960-1973	600-800	139
327-1S	Bed Table	1956-1973	150-300	141
329-1	Suspended Vanity	1960-1973	200-300	140
332	"T" Angle Bench	1956-1971	500-800	119
352 W	Low Conference or Dining Table	1955-1968	350-500	117
355	Coffee Table	1955-1970	150-250	114
358	Coffee Table	1955-1970	200-400	115
360	Plank Top Table	1955-1956	200-400	114
400R	Slat Bench	1951-1971, 1987-1998	900-1500	112
404	"Parallel Bars" Round Coffee Table	1955-1968	300-500	113
405	Parallel Bar Coffee Table	1955-1968	600-900	113
420-2	Side Chair	1952-1998	100-150	58
420-3	Side Chair	1954-1984	100-150	59
420-4	Side Chair	1952-1998	100-150	60
421	Small Diamond Chair	1952-1984, 1987-1998	150-250	75
421-2	Small Diamond Chair	1952-1984, 1987-1998	150-250	76
422	Large Diamond Chair	1954-1979, 1987-1998	400-650	75
423 C	High Back Diamond "Bird Chair"	1952-1984, 1987-1998	550-750	74
424	Diamond Chair Ottoman	1952-1984, 1987-1998	150-250	74
425	Child's Chair	1955-1981, 1983-1984	100-200	60
426	Child's Chair	1955-1975	100-200	60
427	Side Chair	1956-1973	100-150	59
428	Bar Stool	1962-1973, 1983-1998	200-300	62
500 PM	L-Shaped Secretarial Desk	1952-1955	600-800	151
501 PM	L-Shaped Executive Secretarial Desk	1952-1955	600-800	151
502 B- BWM	Small Executive Desk	1952-1955	600-800	151
503 B- BM	Large Executive Desk	1952-1955	800-1200	150
503 A-BM	Large Executive Desk	1952-1955	800-1200	150
1, 503 E	Double Pedestal Desk	1955-1983	400-600	152
503 D-BM	Large Executive Desk	1952-1955	800-1200	150
2, 510 WV	End Table	1958-1976	150-400	125
2, 511 MC	Coffee Table	1958-1976	150-400	125
1, 513 WR	Small Executive Desk	1955-1983	300-500	153
2, 514 MC	End Table	1958-1976	150-400	125
1, 517	Small Executive Desk	1955-1983	600-800	152

Model Number	Description	Production Date	Value	Page
2,518 RW	Coffee Table	1958-1975	150-400	125
1,523 W	Double Pedestal Secretarial Desk	1955-1960?	300-500	153
540	Cabinet	1952-1978	300-400	133
541	Cabinet	1952-1983	350-500	133
1,543 W	Double Pedestal L-Shaped Secretarial Desk	1955-1983	300-500	153
2,562 T	Side Table	1958-1976	150-400	125
3,570 WR	Rectangular Conference Table	1958-1971	200-400	124
1,570 WR	Rectangular Conference Table	1958-1971	250-450	124
575	Sofa	1954-1970	1200-1800	89
576	Sofa	1954-1970	1200-1800	90
2,577 BC	Sofa	1954-1970	1200-1800	90
578	Sofa	1954-1970	1000-1500	89
580	Conference Table	1952-1956	1000-2000	117
1,581	Boat Shaped Conference Table	1958-1976, 1987-1998	1000-2000	118
3,581	Boat Shaped Conference Table	1958-1976	1000-2000	118
600	Cloud Cocktail Table	1945	200-300	96
625 L	Side Table	1945	100-200	96
632 D	Dining Table	1945	200-400	97
638 C	Coffee Table	1945	100-200	97
652 U1/2	Arm Chair	1941-1960	350-500	37
652 W	Arm Chair	1941-1960	350-500	37
652 W2	Settee	1941-1948	1500-2000	38
652 U2 1/2	Settee	1941-1948	1200-1500	38
652 U	Arm Chair	1941-1960	350-500	38
654 L	Chair	1941-1960	600-1200	38
654 U 1/2	Chair	1941-1960	350-500	37
654 W	Chair	1941-1960, 1998	350-500	38
654 U	Chair	1941-1960	350-500	37
655 W	Lounge Chair	1945-1946	450-550	40
655	Lounge Chair	1955-1962	200-400	82

Model Number	Description	Production Date	Value	Page
655 U	Lounge Chair	1945-1946	350-450	39
655 U2	Settee	1945-1946	500-700	42
655 UH	High Back Lounge Chair	1945-1946	350-450	39
656	Settee	1955	600-800	82
657 UH	High Back Rocking Chair	1945-1946	350-450	42
657 W	Rocking Chair	1945-1946	450-550	41
657 U	Rocking Chair	1945-1946	350-450	40
658 U	Sectional Sofa	1945-1946	800-1000	41
658 W	Lounge Chair	1945-1946	450-550	42
666 WSP	Side Chair	1942-1961, 1998-	250-350	36
666 USP	Side Chair	1942-1961	250-350	36
666 UAC	Arm Chair	1946?	250-350	36
666 W	Side Chair	1942-1961, 1998-	250-350	36
666 U	Side Chair	1942-1961	250-350	37
667 W	Webbed Stool	1947?-1958, 1998	200-350	47
676	Sofa	1955-1961	1200-1800	82
700	Daybed	1947-1961	2000-4000	143
701	Convertible Sofa Bed	1950-1954	1500-2000	144
703 BC	Convertible Sofa Bed	1958-1970	2000-3000	145
703 UAC	Arm Chair	1945-1946	200-350	43
703 WSC	Side Chair	1945-1946	150-250	43
704	Single Bed	1950	200-400	142
704 BC	Convertible Sofa Bed with Arms	1958-1970	2000-3000	145
721H	Single Bed	1956-1964	200-500	142
740 WP	Headboard	1956-1968	100-150	141
740	Headboard Series	1956-1970	100-300	141

NA: No Price Available

** Models 129 and 130 are componants of model 128

The following code numbers or letters were used in Knoll model numbers:

ABC-nesting tables
AC-arm chair
BC-brushed chrome
C-caned doors
C-chrome
E-ebony or ebonized
F-1-black plastic laminate top
F-2-white plastic laminate top
GP-grey plastic top
H-highback
L-leather
M-white Italian marble with grey vein
MC-Italian Cremo marble
MW-wallen grey marble
N-Nakashima
NK- Nordiska Kompaniet
PC-polished chrome
Plastic top-Plastic laminate over wood top.
PLB-plastic back

PS-plastic back
R-redwood top
RW-rosewood
S-redwood slat top
S-swivel
SC-side chair
T-wood or teak
U-upholstered
ULB-upholstered back
U1/2- Upholstered separate seat and back
W-webbed
W-wood or walnut
WR-walnut plastic laminate
WS-walnut swivel
W-solid walnut
WV-walnut veneer
W1-hanging cabinet
1/2-half black and half white

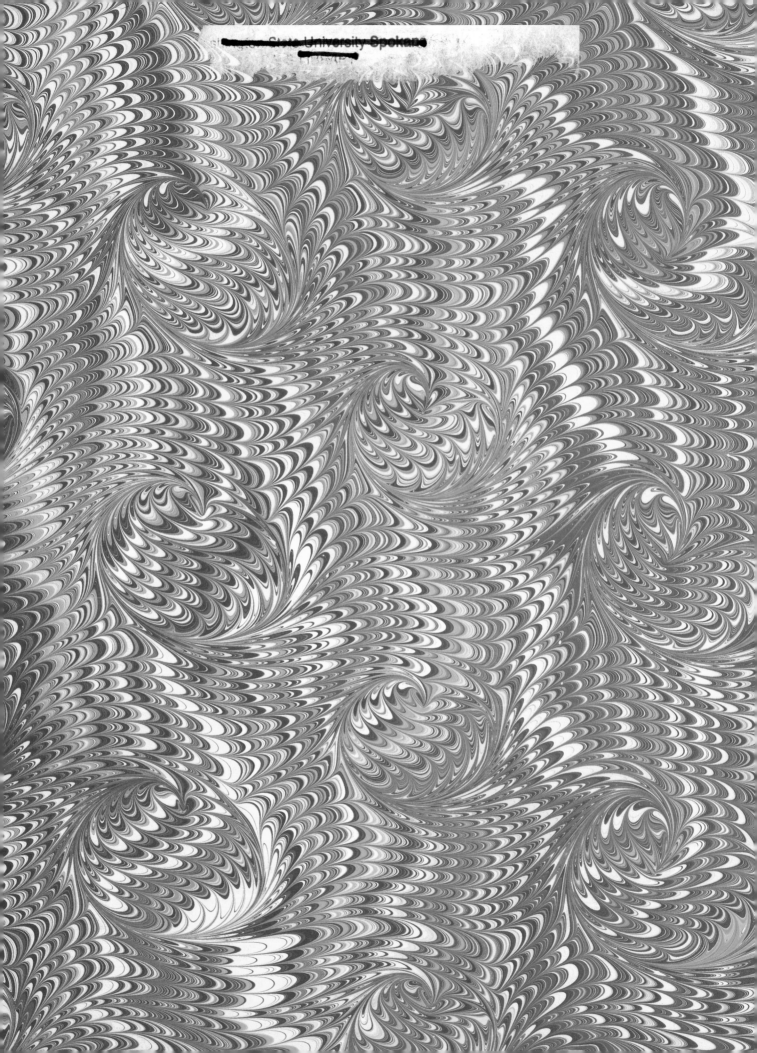